GRETA
Thunberg

Tracey Turner
Illustrations by Tom Knight

Abrams Books for Young Readers
New York

For Toby and his huggable hairy friends, Wellington and Polo. —TT

For anyone who has fought for their beliefs. —TK

The facts in *First Names: Greta Thunberg* have been carefully checked and are accurate to the best of our knowledge, but if you spot something you think may be incorrect please let us know. This text is intended to be entertaining, that's why we've included Greta as a cartoon character. However, the words and thoughts spoken by this character are not the actual words and thoughts of the real Greta Thunberg and the Explained sections aren't explained in Greta Thunberg's own words. Some of the passages in this book are actual quotes from Greta and other important people. You'll be able to tell which ones they are by the style of type: *"I want you to panic. I want you to feel the fear I feel every day."*

Library of Congress Control Number 2021945014

ISBN 978-1-4197-3740-4

Text copyright © 2021 Tracey Turner
Illustrations copyright © 2021 Tom Knight
Book design by Charice Silverman
2021 © as UK edition. First published in 2021
by David Fickling Books Limited

Printed and bound in U.S.A.
10 9 8 7 6 5 4 3 2 1

Abrams Books for Young Readers are available at special discounts when purchased in quantity for premiums and promotions as well as fundraising or educational use. Special editions can also be created to specification. For details, contact specialsales@abramsbooks.com or the address below.

Abrams® is a registered trademark of Harry N. Abrams, Inc.

ABRAMS The Art of Books
195 Broadway, New York, NY 10007
abramsbooks.com

Contents

SKOLSTREJK FÖR KLIMATET

Introduction—Stockholm, Sweden, 2011

Greta sat at her school desk with tears in her eyes.

Each scene on the screen in front of the class was more terrible than the last. In one, a scrawny, miserable-looking polar bear was marooned on a piece of Arctic ice. In another, a giant island made from bits of plastic trash rose and fell with the waves on a blue sea.

The video explained that the island was about the size of Mexico. A floating trash pile the size of a country?

It's too horrible to be true.

The children couldn't believe their eyes, but when the film finished, their teacher told them that it was **all completely true**. "This is why everyone should save energy and recycle things," she said.

"Is there anything else we can do?" asked a girl at the front of the class.

"Not really," said the teacher sadly. "We should all hope someone invents something to make the problem go away." And she told the children how some of the most powerful companies in the world—

oil companies, for example—weren't at all interested in being environmentally friendly because they made most of their money from the fossil fuels that were causing the Arctic ice to melt in the first place.

"Also," she went on, "although scientists have proven that climate change is real, not everyone believes it's true."

Greta was stunned—how could people just "not believe" in science? How could everyone just carry on going to work and school, doing their homework, taking vacations . . . when all the time, **terrible things were happening** to the planet because of climate change, pollution, and plastic waste?

All the children in the classroom were just as shocked and upset as Greta . . .

. . . for about five minutes. Then it was time for recess, and they started heading for the classroom door, chatting, arguing, rushing off to play in the playground.

"Oh, by the way," the teacher added, "I won't be here next week. I'm off to New York for a wedding!'

Some of the kids stopped and crowded around their teacher excitedly. They exchanged stories of vacations they'd had in faraway locations around the world.

Greta couldn't believe it. Had everyone just forgotten the video they'd just watched? How could they talk about flying around the world when they must know that aircraft pollution was making the planet's problems even worse?

Greta didn't rush off happily, chatting, and playing with the rest of her classmates. She was on her own, as usual. She almost always liked to be quiet anyway, but now she was also upset. The video had shown that Planet Earth was in BIG trouble, and she couldn't stop thinking about how awful the situation was. **Why wasn't anyone doing anything about it?**

Tears began to roll down her face. She didn't say anything out loud, but she made a resolution: she was NOT going to forget about this. She was NOT just going to hope someone else would sort out the problem, or that climate change would somehow go away by itself.

I am going to do something about it.

Since the day eight-year-old Greta watched the video about climate change at school, a lot has changed. She's stuck to her word, and she really has done something about it. Now she's known around the world and is one of the most influential people on the planet. Greta:

- Started a global movement for climate change involving millions of people—she's spoken to audiences of thousands!

- Became the youngest person EVER to be nominated for the Nobel Peace Prize—twice!

- Met the Pope, spoke with Leonardo DiCaprio, and went for a bike ride with Arnold Schwarzenegger.

- Led the biggest climate strike in history.

It's not me that's important. It's what we're doing about the climate crisis.

But before we find out what the climate crisis is and how Greta did all these amazing things and affected millions of people, let's travel back to 2003, when Greta was born . . .

1   GRETA'S GREAT START

Long before she started having an effect on the climate change movement, Greta had a big effect on her parents. Life was already pretty good for Mom, Malena Ernman, and Dad, Svante Thunberg, when Greta was born on January 3, 2003. Both parents had successful careers, plenty of money, a comfortable home, and now a new baby—though they also knew they'd have to make some changes to their lifestyle, because babies tend to be quite demanding.

Greta's mom, Malena, was famous in Sweden, where the family lived, thanks to her extraordinary voice. She'd loved singing folk music when she was a child, had switched to jazz after she left college, but really made her name singing opera. As an opera star she performed with some of the world's most talented conductors and orchestras. She'd released a couple of albums, appeared on TV, and played the part of a prince in a film of the short opera, *Die Fledermaus*.

Greta's dad, Svante, came from a family of actors and had followed his parents onto the stage. He'd performed in some of Sweden's top theaters and done some TV and film work too. But when he was offered his dream job, a TV comedy series, **he turned it down**! Malena was pregnant, and they both knew that her career was far more successful than Svante's, and that she could earn loads more money than he could. So Svante decided he was the one who would take time off to look after their new baby.

With Dad as her main caretaker, life started out pretty well for baby Greta. She lived with her parents in the beautiful city of Stockholm, Sweden's capital, which is built on fourteen islands where Lake Mälaren meets the Baltic Sea. The family had an apartment in the city and a summer house on the nearby island of Ingarö. When Malena had to travel for her work, **Svante and Greta went along for the ride**, settling in different cities around Europe— Berlin, Paris, Amsterdam—for two months at a time.

Things got even better in 2005, when Malena had another daughter, Beata, and Greta gained a little sister. While the girls were small, the family of four carried on travelling happily together, staying in smart apartments, visiting parks and zoos, and playing together at home whenever Malena's rehearsal schedules allowed.

Song Contests

In 2009, when Greta was six, her mom entered *Melodifestivalen*, Sweden's most popular TV show, a singing competition that's a bit like *American Idol*. Though Malena was already a big name in opera before she entered, the competition quickly made her **even more famous**. She won first place and the honor of representing her country in that year's Eurovision Song Contest.

Eurovision was held in Moscow, and Malena interrupted her busy opera schedule to take part. She performed the Swedish entry in French and English (she'd helped write the bilingual lyrics herself), to an audience of 122 million people around the world, looking stunningly beautiful in a long white dress.

It's Mommy!

Malena's song didn't win Eurovision. In fact, it came a disappointing 21st place out of 25. Malena did wonder if this might have something to do with her tweets in support of an LGBTQ+ protest march that was happening in Moscow at the same time as the song contest. A Pride march had been banned by the Russian government, and Malena was outraged. The only other contestant who supported the protest on social media was the Spanish contestant, and she came 24th! But if Malena cared about her disappointing ranking, she didn't show it, and she must have felt a bit better when **her song reached number one** in the Swedish Svensktoppen radio chart.

Even now that she is really famous, Malena isn't the sort of celebrity who goes to premieres and fancy parties. Once a show is over, she usually hurries home, not just because she loves her family, but also because she's quite a shy person—singing on stage is fine, but socializing isn't much fun for Malena.

High Flyers

Before Greta became a world-changing climate activist, both Malena and Svante would have said they cared about the environment too. They certainly **wanted to do the right thing**. But, like most people, they thought that governments basically had the climate crisis under control, so ordinary people didn't need to worry about it too much. They recycled, avoided single-use plastics when they could, and that sort of thing. In other words, they were like most people in rich countries around the world: keen to do what they could to help the environment—when they remembered to think about it. But generally they didn't think about it very much.

Before Greta learned about climate change

Hurry up, we need to stop at the shops on the way to the airport.

Let's go out for a steak when we get there!

9

Between 2000 and 2014, Malena traveled by plane to Belgium, Austria, France, England, Germany, Spain, Japan, and the United States, among other countries, performing in operas and concerts and appearing on TV. It was a glamorous life, and especially fun when the family came too. But **Malena's career was about to change**, and all because of her eldest daughter.

Both Greta and Beata are very clever. Beata is a talented musician like her mother and happiest when she's singing or dancing (and especially if she's singing or dancing to Little Mix, her absolute favorite band). Greta has a photographic memory, which means she only has to look at something once to hold the information in her head, without needing to really work at remembering it. She knows all the world's capital cities forwards and backwards!

With a memory like that, you won't be surprised to hear that Greta did well in school. But she didn't always enjoy being at school. She was a bit different from the other children, and she found making friends especially difficult, which is another reason why she was so often on her own.

In class, teachers had told Greta that she should always turn off lights and never leave the tap running when she brushed her teeth to save energy and water. They explained a bit about climate change, but at first Greta didn't think it could really be true—if it was, then surely everyone in the world would be talking about nothing else, and spending most of their time trying to do something about it.

I didn't know much about climate change back then.

But the day Greta's teacher showed the film with the island of plastic and the polar bears, she realized that **climate change was actually real**, and that—astonishingly—no one seemed to be doing that much about it. Like her teacher, whenever most people did give it any thought they ended up shaking their heads sadly, turning off a light or a tap, or passing the buck to the children, saying "Your generation will be the ones who save the planet."

> But how can we save the world? We're just children.

Greta really WAS upset about climate change. Once she'd realized how desperate the situation was, she couldn't just ignore it and carry on as normal. Instead, she decided to use her considerable skills and intelligence to find out all about it . . .

2   GRETA BECOMES AN EXPERT

Greta started reading, watching, and studying everything she could get her hands on to do with climate change.

It wasn't long before she was an expert.

CLIMATE CHANGE: THE BASICS, EXPLAINED

There are gases in the Earth's atmosphere that keep in heat, like how the glass in a greenhouse keeps plants warm, and we can't live without those gases. "Greenhouse gases," including carbon dioxide (CO_2) and methane (CH_4), keep our planet at the right temperature for us to live.

BUT the more greenhouse gases there are in the atmosphere, the hotter Earth gets.

The Greenhouse Effect

Energy from the Sun warms Earth and is absorbed by its surface.

But Earth reflects some energy from the Sun back into space.

Greenhouse gases absorb energy from the Sun too, so that less of it is reflected into space, kind of like a blanket making Earth's surface warmer.

The more greenhouses gases there are in the atmosphere, the more heat is sent back down to the surface of Earth.

Earth's climate has changed naturally over time. But, in the last 200 years there's been a very sharp rise in temperatures that definitely hasn't been natural.

200 years ago

150 years ago

200 years ago the Industrial Revolution had started, and more and more coal was being burned to make steam for machines.

Climate scientists compare CO_2 levels today with "preindustrial levels"— this means the levels of CO_2 in the atmosphere between the years 1850 and 1900—to work out how much they have increased.

The temperature rise is NOT a coincidence.

The gas, oil, and coal that we use to drive our cars, and heat, power, and light our homes and factories, all come from fossil fuels.

Animals and plants that were alive millions of years ago died.

Over time they were covered in sediment.

And over hundreds of millions of years they form the fuels we rely on today.

Anything that's alive, or has been alive, contains carbon, and when fossil fuels burn, the carbon they contain is released and sent back into the atmosphere as CO_2.

Tiny particles of carbon are also released, causing pollution.

The fact is, it's human activities — especially the ones that involve fossil fuels—that are increasing the greenhouse gases in the atmosphere and making the world warmer.

Today, nearly all of us use energy all the time, and an astonishing **84%** of it **still** comes from fossil fuels!

More than half of the fossil-fuel energy we use comes from power plants and factories.

A third is used by different kinds of transportation—cars, trucks, ships, and planes.

When you turn on a light you could be burning fossil fuels.

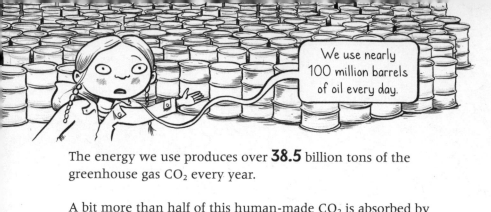

The energy we use produces over **38.5** billion tons of the greenhouse gas CO_2 every year.

A bit more than half of this human-made CO_2 is absorbed by Earth's plant life and oceans.

The rest hangs around in Earth's atmosphere along with the CO_2 coming from natural sources that are already there.

It isn't going away any time soon— the gas will stay in the atmosphere for hundreds or possibly even thousands of years!

Compared with pre-industrial levels (1850–1900), the extra greenhouse gases in the atmosphere have made Earth's temperature rise by about 1.8°F on average across the world. It doesn't sound like much, but we're already seeing the consequences of the increase in temperature. It's caused:

- Glaciers and sea ice to melt, so sea levels have risen.
- Animals and plants to go extinct.
- Natural disasters—fires, floods, droughts, and extreme weather, such as hurricanes and tornadoes.

All these things are happening more now than they've ever happened in the whole of human history.

It sounds dreadful, but there is a solution. If we stopped burning fossil fuels and adding to the greenhouse gases in the atmosphere, we could halt global warming and avoid the worst consequences.

All we have to do is to wake up and change.

Unfortunately, changing our way of life isn't that easy!

GRETA'S CLEVER RELATIVE

Today there are many scientists investigating climate change. But, by a **strange coincidence**, one of the very first was a member of Greta's own family. Greta's dad, Svante, is named after a distant, long-dead relative, Svante Arrhenius, a scientist who won a Nobel Prize for Chemistry in 1903.

Before he won his Nobel Prize, Arrhenius had already made the discovery he's most famous for.

He'd studied the work of John Tyndall, one of the first scientists to identify greenhouse gases, and then made his own calculations that burning fossil fuels would lead to a warmer climate.

When levels of CO_2 in the atmosphere rise, it causes an increase in the surface temperature of Earth.

He realized, even then, that industrialization was putting more greenhouse gases into the atmosphere because it used fossil fuels, and that **the world was getting hotter** as a result. In 1896 he published a paper about it with the catchy title:

ON THE INFLUENCE OF CARBONIC ACID* IN THE AIR UPON THE TEMPERATURE OF THE GROUND

But this was before cars and planes had anything to do with it. When Arrhenius was writing, it was coal that was causing most of the warming. He calculated that . . .

*"Carbonic acid" is what people used to call CO_2 (but it means something quite different today and is used in carbonated drinks, cosmetics, fertilizers, and more).

Arrhenius thought an increase in temperature in Sweden would be great for the country!

He also reckoned it would take **two thousand years** for CO_2 in the atmosphere to reach the level it's at today, because the amount of fossil fuels we burn today was completely unimaginable to a scientist working 100 years ago.

Amazingly, Arrhenius's formula for working out how much the temperature will rise in relation to the amount of CO_2 in the atmosphere **is still used by climate scientists today.**

So let's give Greta's brilliant relative a massive round of applause. It's a shame no one really paid much attention to his findings at the time. But then, like Arrhenius, they probably didn't think they had anything to worry about yet.

Over the years, as more and more CO_2 was released into the atmosphere from cars and planes, factories, homes and power stations, Earth did very gradually begin to get warmer, just as Svante Arrhenius had predicted. But it wasn't until the 1970s, when people started to worry about the greenhouse effect and the production of greenhouse gases, that they looked at Arrhenius's formula again.

Has Anyone Been Doing Anything About Climate Change?

Greta was horrified by what she was finding out. But when she realized that people had known about the negative effects of global warming for at least thirty years, and **governments hadn't done anything about it**, she was angry.

This problem could have been solved, but instead it's gotten worse! The older generations are stealing my generation's future.

GLOBAL WARMING

CLIMATE CHANGE THE SCIENCE

Twentieth-century Climate Change Timeline

Every so often during the twentieth century people had thought about doing something about climate change:

1956—A *New York Times* article said: "*Warmer Climate on the Earth May be Due to More Carbon Dioxide in the Air.*" But it argued that, because coal and oil were plentiful and cheap, it would be difficult to tackle the problem.

1979—The first World Climate Conference was held in Geneva where scientists agreed that CO_2 emissions needed to be reduced. Later an Intergovernmental Panel on Climate Change (IPCC) was formed. But governments around the world took no notice.

In fact, they allowed CO_2 emissions to get even worse.

1988—As a result of droughts, fires, and record temperatures, the greenhouse effect made the headlines. Scientists worked out how much they thought Earth was likely to warm up and warned:

We should take action now, or things will get worse and go beyond a point of no return.

Yeah, yeah, whatever . . .

Climate scientist James Hansen told the United States Congress it was 99% certain that global warming was caused by an increase of CO_2 and other greenhouse gases in the atmosphere. Still, nothing was done. James is still a climate activist today.

1992—The United Nations set up a conference on the environment in Rio de Janeiro, Brazil. This "Earth Summit" was the largest environmental conference that had ever been held. Over 30,000 people attended, including 117 heads of state—no conference had ever drawn so many world leaders together. In all, 178 countries were represented. Surely this would make a difference!

THE YOUNGEST DELEGATE AT THE EARTH SUMMIT

Nearly seven thousand miles away, in Vancouver, Canada, four children had set up their own environmental group. Hearing about the summit, they decided that one of them had to be there. They raised the money themselves and sent Severn Cullis-Suzuki to deliver a speech to that enormous audience. She was only twelve years old!

Be sure to tell them what we think, Severn.

You bet I will.

Just like Greta, Severn spoke for children and generations to come and gave the adults a good scolding for not doing anything about the environment, animal extinction, pollution, and greenhouse gases.

Talking to the audience not as politicians, but as parents, siblings, and friends, she said:

EARTH SUMMIT

All this is happening before our eyes and yet we act as if we have all the time we want and all the solutions . . .

Severn was saying this nearly thirty years ago! It makes me so mad that almost nothing has changed!

Tell me about it!

Severn today

The conference delegates were clearly moved, and the speech is still watched online today. Maybe if social media had existed back in the 1990s, Severn would have become famous, like Greta. But since her speech all those years ago, CO_2 emissions have just kept on going up and up, and she has never been able to stop campaigning.

In 2019, Glen Peters, a Norwegian scientist studying the rise of CO_2 levels in the atmosphere, found out something grim. Between 1870 and the present day, half the rise in CO_2 levels had come from emissions made by human activity **just in the past thirty years**.

So, why wasn't (and isn't) anyone making the far-reaching changes that are needed? The main problem was (and is) money. Massive piles of it.

An oil company has a very obvious interest in keeping things the way they are. It wants everyone to carry on driving gasoline cars and making electricity from oil-fired power stations—otherwise, it wouldn't be in business. And then where would it get its **huge amounts of cash**?

A hamburger restaurant chain happily clears areas of carbon-absorbing rainforest to graze the cattle that go into its burgers because that's the cheapest way to get their meat, and they want to carry on making **massive piles of money**.

Companies that don't want to do anything to stop climate change spend a lot of time **spreading rumors** that climate change isn't real, and persuading governments to keep them in business. And they're really good at it! They're at least partly to blame for why many people don't realize that the situation is as bad as it actually is, and why governments continue spending money on coal- and oil-fired power stations instead of investing in renewable energy.

If you're thinking that things can't be all that bad, I'm here to tell you they really are.

THE DIRE CONSEQUENCES OF NOT DOING ANYTHING

If the warming carries on, and we don't act now, these are just a few of the very bad things that are likely to happen (on top of the things that have happened already):

🌳 Over the next twenty to forty years as temperatures rise there could be summers in the Arctic with no ice at all. And all that melted ice will make sea levels rise even further.

🌳 And as sea levels rise people living in low-lying areas will be forced out of their homes, because of flooding. There will be more and more climate refugees.

🌳 There will also be more and more animal extinctions when habitats are changed or lost as a result of climate change.

🌳 Unable to survive in warming waters, coral reefs in the oceans could die.

🌳 Trees in the Amazon that currently absorb CO_2 will die back or be burned in forest fires that are caused by rising temperatures, increasing the rate of warming. There will be no going back after that.

Reading and understanding all these things when she was so young was devastating for Greta. At the age of eleven, she became seriously depressed.

3   GRETA GRADUALLY GETS BETTER

No wonder Greta was unhappy. The facts were, and still are, tremendously upsetting. It seemed unlikely people were just going to stop flying in planes or driving their cars, and factories weren't going to just shut down overnight. But the good news was that there was still time to do something about it—and there still is.

At first, Greta didn't know what she could do. She knew she wanted to be part of the solution, but she was just one very small person. **And how could one very small person possibly make a difference?**

Because of her depression, Greta cried a lot. She found sleeping difficult, which made her feel even worse. She stopped doing things she enjoyed, like playing the piano and riding her bike. She'd always been quiet, but now she spoke less and less, and she also ate less and less food. At one point she lost twenty pounds in just two months.

Depression is more than just feeling sad, it's an illness that can stop people from doing the things they normally would. Among other things, it might make someone feel very tired, find sleeping difficult or, as happened with Greta, lose interest in things they used to enjoy. Lots of people experience depression, and it happens for all sorts of reasons, and it can take time to go away, but sufferers often find it helps to talk to a sympathetic friend, relative, or doctor.

Dreadful School Days

Unfortunately, Greta didn't have friends at school to confide in, and she carried on crying a lot and not speaking or eating while she was there. The teachers were concerned, but they didn't know what to do, so they started calling her dad and asking him to come and take Greta home. At least when she was there she could sit and cuddle the family dog.

Moses, their golden retriever, was a very important member of the family and always a **huge comfort** to Greta.

Dogs are wonderful. They're always your best friend, they never judge, and they're always up for a big hug.

Moses listens to every word I say and completely agrees with me.

Dogs also love leftovers— no food need ever be wasted with them.

Later on, in 2018, when Greta was fifteen, the family expanded to include another member, a black Labrador rescue dog named Roxy.

For anyone like Greta who's shy, quiet, doesn't make friends very easily, and finds school a bit overwhelming, having a furry friend to rely on can be the **best thing ever**.

But despite the hugs from Moses, things didn't get any better, and after a while, Malena, Svante, and Beata were the only people Greta spoke to. She was hardly eating anything at all. One time at breakfast she only managed to eat a third of a banana. It took her 53 minutes.

Greta couldn't stop thinking about climate change and other things that were wrong with the world. She wondered whether there was any future for the kids her age. Because she was hardly speaking, she kept a lot of her worries and despair to herself. Moses continued to be a real comfort, but he was, after all, a dog, and didn't have anything very helpful to say about climate science.

On the days when Greta did manage to get to school, she had another reason to be unhappy: she was being bullied.

Other kids ignored and avoided her some of the time, and the rest of the time they would point and laugh at her, push her over in the playground, and call her names. When she could, she took refuge in the library or hid in the bathroom. No one stood up for her. She felt completely alone.

Greta didn't tell her parents about the bullies, either; she kept the horrible situation at school to herself. Not sharing her worries must have made everything so much worse. Greta desperately needed to talk to someone she could trust.

One evening, Svante came to Greta's school for a Christmas celebration. As he walked down the corridor with his daughter he couldn't believe what he saw. The other children didn't even try to hide what they were doing—they pointed and laughed at Greta, while her dad was walking right beside her! Finally, over the holiday break, Greta began telling her parents what had been happening, and **they were horrified**.

Svante and Malena wanted to hear what the school had to say about it. After all, bullying is always hurtful and can do damage that lasts a lifetime. The school's reaction, however, was nothing like Greta's parents were hoping for. The teachers freely admitted that they knew about the bullying, but they reckoned it was happening because Greta didn't say hello, sometimes behaved oddly, and stood out as being different from the other children—they thought she'd brought it on herself!

Svante and Malena couldn't believe it. Their clever, funny, wonderful daughter was being bullied every day she went to school, and the people who were supposed to be protecting her thought that this was, basically, OK.

Malena and Svante complained to the Swedish Schools Inspectorate (a government agency that helps with school improvement and development), and Greta didn't go back to the school. She did stay in contact with one kind teacher, however, who gave up her spare time to give Greta **private lessons in the school library**. Luckily, the teacher was another person Greta felt able to speak to.

Eventually Greta transferred schools, but for a while she stayed at home. Svante and Malena were beside themselves with worry. Greta still wasn't eating much more than tiny amounts of avocado, rice, and gnocchi, and her parents thought she might be suffering from anorexia—an illness that makes some people stop eating because they think they're overweight even though they aren't.

Greta's lack of appetite was certainly making her dangerously ill. But when a doctor finally told her she'd have to go into hospital and be fed by a drip if she didn't start eating more, Greta **made a huge effort**. She started eating pancakes, and even though she was still eating very little, it was enough.

GUESTS IN THE SUMMER HOUSE

Svante and Malena had always done what they could to help good causes, and they were very concerned about refugees. Since 2011, a civil war had been raging in Syria (and still is) after protesters tried to overthrow the government. Bombs, gunfire, and chemical weapons had killed thousands of people. The situation was so bad that many Syrians had decided to take the difficult and dangerous decision to leave the country, rather than staying and risking being killed. Altogether, 5.6 million Syrians left because of the war.

Greta and her family read the terrible news of what was happening in Syria and **wanted to help**. Malena had spoken out in support of refugees before, and now she urged the Swedish government to offer aid to Syrian refugees. She was prepared to give her own time and money, but Beata and Greta persuaded both their parents to go one step further.

We're lucky enough to have a summer house—it's empty most of the time.

A refugee family could live in it!

That's how a Syrian family who had fled from Damascus came to move into their house on the island of Ingarö. Greta's family helped to arrange bus passes and food supplies, and over the year the Syrian family spent at the summer house, the two families got to know each other well. At the weekends they would all spend time together, and the Syrian family made delicious dinners for them all.

SOME BIG CHANGES

Quietly, Greta had started taking her own steps towards making sure she wasn't contributing to climate change. One of the most important things she did was **stop eating meat**, and then dairy and other animal products. Greta still wasn't eating a lot, and you might think limiting her diet even more would be a big problem for someone who hadn't been getting enough food in the first place. But as long as the food was nutritious and Greta ate enough of it, becoming vegan wasn't a problem.

CHANGING YOUR DIET TO SAVE THE PLANET, EXPLAINED

I love animals and don't want them to suffer, and animals bred for food are sometimes treated badly. That's one reason for not eating them, but there are plenty more.

A report from the IPCC says that if people cut down on the amount of meat (especially beef and lamb) and dairy they eat, more people around the world could be fed using less land.

Meat and dairy production contributes to global warming. Animals such as cows and sheep eat grass, which is very tough and difficult to digest. As a result they spend a lot of time burping (and farting) methane.

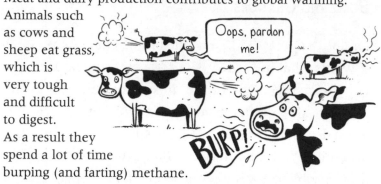

Oops, pardon me!

BURP!

Methane is a greenhouse gas that's even worse for climate change than CO_2. **Farm animals produce about 14.5% of the world's greenhouse-gas emissions each year.**

In rich countries, people eat far more meat than they need to! In many places, natural forests that used to provide a home for animals, birds, and insects are cleared, so that enormous cattle farms can be constructed to keep up with the huge demand.

On average people in Nigeria eat around 13 lbs of meat a year. On average people in America eat more than 16 times that amount!

You eat that much meat?

Additionally, trees are often cleared to grow soya that's fed to cows, sheep, pigs, and chickens. But trees absorb CO_2, which is one of the many reasons we need more of them.

We should be planting more trees, not chopping them down.

With fewer cows and sheep in the world, more land could be available for trees and other plants to regrow.

Meat production also uses tons of resources. One estimate says it takes 50 bathfuls of water to get just one beef steak onto a plate!

WHAT YOU CAN DO: Cutting down on meat (especially beef and lamb) and dairy can help make a difference.

Eating a more plant-based diet isn't that hard. Why not give it a try for one or two days a week?

Teaching Mom and Dad

Even though she wasn't talking to anyone else, Greta did talk to her family about the climate crisis and the environment—a lot. Malena and Svante told her to try and stop worrying, and that everything would be OK. They were trying to help, but Greta knew that **they were completely wrong**—if no one did anything, everything would most definitely not be OK.

So Greta began her campaign to convince her parents that Planet Earth was heading for disaster unless people did something about it. She took every chance she could to keep them up to speed with the climate crisis.

She didn't give up, and she proved to be **very persuasive**. Malena, Svante, and Beata really started to listen. Eventually, the whole family became vegan too—except for Malena, who's still working on it. And before long, everyone in the family was becoming an expert on climate change—well, maybe not the dog. Once they had all the information, they realized they had to make some more serious lifestyle changes.

They Stopped Buying So Much Stuff

🌳 Clothes shopping soon became a thing of the past for the Thunberg-Ernman family. People are buying more clothes and keeping them for less time than ever before. A shocking 85% of all textiles are thrown away every year.

> The equivalent of one garbage truck full of used clothing is dumped in landfill or burned every second!

🌳 Around the world, clothing factories use tons of power and water. The chemicals in fabric dyes are big water polluters, and clothes sent to landfill take a very long time to break down.

🌳 Almost every time anything is made, greenhouse gases are released into the atmosphere—for example: a new bicycle means metal has to be dug out of the ground, energy is used to construct it, and the finished bike has to be shipped from wherever it was made.

So the family made a decision to look after the things they already had and to keep them as long as possible. If they really needed to buy something new, they bought the best they could afford so that it would last a long time. **They didn't find it easy!** But if someone in the family tried to buy anything and sneak it home, somehow Greta always knew.

Have you been shopping again?

Er . . .

Let me see your receipts.

RECYCLING, EXPLAINED

You might have heard the expression REDUCE, REUSE, RECYCLE. The most important words are REDUCE and REUSE. It's good to recycle too, but there are still some problems:

Most rich countries produce more waste than they can process at home, so the trash and recycling is sent abroad.

Every day, households in the UK produce about 1.1kg of waste. US households produce nearly twice as much. In the UK, 45% of this trash goes in recycling bins; in the United States, it's 35%—but in both countries the trash could still be burned or dumped!

While most plastics can be recycled, many aren't, because it's an expensive and complicated process.

Sometimes waste is burned in the country that "recycled" it, because the country can't cope with the amount of recycling, or it's too expensive to process. Sometimes recycling is sent to another country and still ends up being burned to get rid of it. Burning is seen as better than dumping trash in dumps or landfills, because dumps emit methane and can leach toxic chemicals. But burning can release pollution into the atmosphere too.

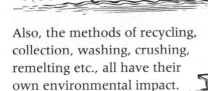

Also, the methods of recycling, collection, washing, crushing, remelting etc., all have their own environmental impact.

WHAT YOU CAN DO: Use refillable cups and bottles and shop in zero-waste stores if you can. Look for companies that are making reusable glass or metal packaging that can be refilled and reused many times.

They Switched to an Electric Car

As well as reducing what they bought, the family got rid of their gas-guzzling car, and they could afford to replace it with an electric one. But because it still needs power, which might be generated from fossil fuels, they only use the car **when they really need to**. Otherwise they walk or bike (generating a total of zero greenhouse gas emissions).

See, we don't really need a car!

No More Flying

There's no doubt that flights are bad for Planet Earth—they produce more greenhouse gases per mile than any other form of transportation. But it gets even worse than that. As well as releasing CO_2 from burning fuel, plane engines produce:

🌳 water vapor (another greenhouse gas)

🌳 soot (tiny particles of carbon that pollute the atmosphere).

Water vapor and soot make the trails planes sometimes leave behind them in the sky, and it's thought that these add to the greenhouse effect. Altogether, scientists think a plane's impact on the climate is more than twice as high as its CO_2 emissions, which are quite bad enough to begin with.

Some languages have a word for the guilt people often feel when they fly somewhere, knowing they're contributing to climate change. In Dutch it's *vliegschaamte*, in German it's *Flugscham*, and in Swedish it's *flygskam*.

In English you might call it "flight shame"

DICTIONARY

Malena certainly felt guilty about flying. Faced with the facts, even though it meant giving up her hugely successful career, she decided to stop flying altogether. She **sang her last opera** in 2014 and started performing in musicals instead, which meant she could stay local and didn't need to travel all over the world.

A few months later, Beata was having a hard time and Svante took her on vacation to Sardinia as a special treat. Greta was not impressed . . .

ARRIVALS

You just released 2.7 tons of CO_2— the annual emissions of five people in Senegal!

Did you enjoy your trip?

CARBON FOOTPRINTS, EXPLAINED

Everyone in the world has a carbon footprint—that's the amount of CO_2 released into the atmosphere every year because of the things we do.

> Events, companies, and products all have carbon footprints too.

A person's carbon footprint varies massively from country to country. It can include how much people buy, eat, and throw away, and the energy they use and where it comes from. In Europe, for example, energy is more likely to come from a renewable source than it is in the United States.

Throughout the world, the average carbon footprint is **5.3** tons per person. But:

🌳 An average Australian, American or Canadian has a carbon footprint of over 16.5 tons per year (around three times the world average CO_2 emissions!).

🌳 The average carbon footprint in the African countries Chad and Niger is only 0.1 tons per year.

🌳 The carbon footprint of 154 people from Chad or Niger is the same as one Australian!

WHAT YOU CAN DO: Visit a website to calculate your carbon footprint—like epa.gov/carbon-footprint-calculator—then work on lowering it, for example, by taking trips by car, avoiding plane flights, riding a bike or taking public transportation whenever possible. Also, try not to waste anything, and buy clothes second hand.

Svante couldn't argue with Greta's facts. He and Malena had realized that **the climate crisis was more important than flying**, and all the other things they had changed in their lives. They also knew how much this meant to their eldest daughter. By not flying they weren't just helping the planet; they were helping her.

Having her family listen to what she was saying showed Greta that she could make a difference. And that made her start to feel better. She realized that most people weren't living the way they did because they didn't care, or were terrible people. Just like her own family, they had no idea how bad the climate crisis was. If she'd succeeded in persuading her own family about climate change, maybe she could try to change other people's minds too?

But unfortunately for Greta and for all of us, we need more than just lifestyle change. It's the world's 100 biggest companies, which account for most of the world's carbon emissions, that should really be making the changes. Governments' policies allow them to keep going. We need to make life changes, but we also need to keep putting pressure on companies and on governments to make the **big changes** that will really make a difference.

If we all adapt our lives and keep putting pressure on the governments and big business, we will make change happen.

No News Is Bad News

One major reason why not many people knew the extent of the climate crisis was because it was hardly ever reported in the news, and Greta could prove it. She counted up all the articles about climate change in the four main Swedish newspapers. It wasn't difficult —there were hardly any! But there were lots of positive articles about things that contributed to climate change, like new cars and trips abroad.

When one of the newspapers announced a climate campaign, Greta's hopes soared. She followed it closely —and was horrified to see that the paper still gave nearly **sixty times more space** to articles on shopping, cars, and air travel than it did to the climate crisis!

With ads all over the place trying to get everyone to buy new stuff, or go on vacation, it was no wonder people didn't realize they were in the middle of a crisis that would affect the future of humanity.

Greta began to realize that there was something positive she could do about climate change. She could make sure people got the message about what was happening to the planet. The more she thought about it, the more **it gave her hope**. It was an answer at last, and today she has something to say to anyone who feels hopeless in the face of the climate crisis:

Act. Do something. Because that is the best medicine against sadness and depression.

Luckily, it turned out that way for Greta.

4   Greta Discovers Her Superpowers

While Greta was busy educating her family about the climate crisis, her parents were making appointments for her with various doctors to see if they could help with her depression and eating issues. A psychologist at Greta's school had mentioned to Malena and Svante that she thought Greta might be on the autism spectrum and, finally, one of the doctors the family was seeing confirmed that this was true.

Greta was diagnosed with Asperger's syndrome. It's a bit confusing since different countries use different terms that mean the same thing, and depending on where Greta lived in the world she might have instead been diagnosed with autistic spectrum disorder, or autistic spectrum condition. Asperger's is a form of autism, but some autistic people don't like using that term.

I'm fine with Asperger's.

Autistic people experience the world differently from most other people because of the way our brains are wired.

Not everyone's brain is the same, of course! But some people share similar differences. As well as autism, other examples of this "neurodiversity" are:

🌳 Attention deficit hyperactivity disorder (ADHD), where people have problems with attention and staying still.

🌳 Obsessive compulsive disorder (OCD), which can make people anxious and have thoughts that lead them to repeat the same actions over and over again.

Sometimes people can have several of these conditions all at once. Greta also has a diagnosis of OCD. Her mom has ADHD, and Beata has ADHD and other conditions including misophonia, which is extreme sensitivity to certain sounds—it's what gives Beata her amazing talent for music.

Autism isn't an illness, and people don't "recover" from it. You can't tell whether someone's autistic just by looking at them. All autistic people are different from one another, just like all non-autistic people aren't the same. Some autistic people see autism as a disability, some see it as a difference. Greta has her own take on it . . .

Greta
@GretaThunberg
I have Asperger's and that means I'm sometimes a bit different from the norm. And—given the right circumstances – being different is a superpower.
#aspiepower

There's no doubt that there are advantages and disadvantages that come from being autistic. But, in general, autistic people might:

🌳 Have a strong sense of justice.

I tend to see things in black and white, right and wrong.

🌳 Worry a lot.

I hate making small talk.

🌳 Find talking with other people difficult.

🌳 Have interests that they're extremely passionate about. (You've probably figured out what Greta's passionate about already!)

🌳 Find it easy to focus and not be distracted, especially if they're focusing on their passion.

🌳 Have no problem at all with public speaking.

There are autistic people in all walks of life, including musicians, film stars, scientists, inventors, and politicians.

The world can be difficult for autistic people, because it's arranged to suit non-autistic people. But one thing's for sure: The world needs people who think differently. And Greta certainly does that.

What Non-autistic People Sometimes Think About Autistic People

> So what's your special talent? Math or computer science?

> Grrr!

Sometimes people say that autistic people don't experience the same feelings as non-autistic people, or don't understand other people's feelings. This isn't true; it's just that autistic people might not show their feelings in the same way. It's even been argued that autistic people feel things MORE strongly than most other people. We've already seen how intense Greta's feelings were, and the effect they had on her.

If you're going to be a world-famous climate activist, it really does seem as though being autistic is a big advantage in some ways. Greta says that because she's not really interested in socializing or other distractions, she's free to concentrate on the things that really matter to her.

> *If I would have been normal like everyone else, I could just continue like everyone else and get stuck in the social game, and just continue like before. But since I was different, I see the world from a different perspective.*

THE PARIS AGREEMENT

Ever since the Earth Summit in Rio (see p. 24), regular United Nations Conferences have been held on climate change. In 2015, when Greta was twelve, there was one in Paris, France. It was known as COP21—COP stands for Conference Of the Parties, and the 21 part means that it was the 21st COP. **Over 40,000** delegates attended, representing **195 countries** around the world, and they included the world's most powerful leaders.

Barack Obama
President of the
United States

Nerendra Modi
Prime Minister of India

Xi Jinping
President of China

The countries came together to agree rules on climate change that they would all have to follow.

Getting nearly 200 countries to agree to anything was never going to be easy. Each delegate wanted the best for their own people, and discussions often went on through the night, as **arguments raged**, sometimes over a single word.

Greta followed what was happening at the conference with keen interest, and a lot of it made her happy. The fact that so many countries had managed to come to an agreement was huge progress, and there were other high points:

🌳 India was persuaded not to build the 400 new coal-fired power stations it had been planning, and to build solar-power ones instead.

🌳 Some of the countries most at risk from rising sea levels joined together to make a request.

Can we aim to limit global warming to a 2.7°F increase instead of 3.6°F that has been suggested, please?

One effect of climate change is absolutely certain: sea levels will rise. In fact, they already have risen by 8 in since about 1870—and 3 in of that has happened over the last 25 years!

Increased global temperatures cause rising sea levels for two reasons.

Firstly, most of the heat caused by the extra greenhouse gases in the atmosphere is absorbed by the oceans. As water heats up, it also expands.

Secondly, the warming atmosphere is causing ice to melt at the poles, and this meltwater pours from glaciers and ice sheets into the sea.

If we don't do something about it, the IPCC estimates that sea levels will rise another 30 in by 2100. This would mean:

🌳 Terrible floods will hit low-lying countries like Bangladesh and the Netherlands, as well as islands of the Pacific and Indian Oceans.

🌳 Cities near the coast, such as Miami, Melbourne, Tokyo and Venice will all be affected too.

🌳 Flooding would cause many millions of people to lose their homes, animals would lose their habitats, drinking water would be contaminated with salt, and salty soil would make it difficult for crops to grow.

We have to make governments TAKE ACTION NOW to prevent this.

So it was good news that the United Nations did agree to the Pacific Island leaders' proposal on limiting the temperature rise. The agreement was signed early in 2016 and Greta looked forward to seeing all the changes that would be made to reduce carbon emissions as a result.

If the world's countries only carry on as they are doing, we are on track for at least 5.4°F degrees of warming before the end of the century.

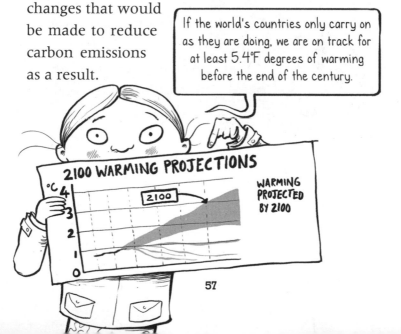

2100 WARMING PROJECTIONS

°C

4
3
2
1
0

2100

WARMING PROJECTED BY 2100

However, if no changes were made after the Paris Agreement, a 2.7°F increase in temperature would probably happen at some point between 2030 and 2052, with a best guess of 2040.

What a Difference a Degree Makes

Half a degree to one degree might sound too small to be important, but don't be fooled. Because Earth's temperature has increased so much since preindustrial levels, scientists have a good idea of what the extra 0.9°F rise will mean. And **it is pretty horrifying**.

After the Paris Agreement, a special report by the IPCC looked at how keeping the temperature rise below 3.6°F would affect the planet. Dozens of authors and editors were involved in preparing it, and they used more than 6,000 scientific contributions from thousands of experts around the world. There was no way anyone could say it wasn't well researched.

I got ahold of the report and made some notes.

These are just a few things Greta found out. . .

🌳 A rise of about another 1.8°F above current levels would bring more deadly heatwaves, wildfires and droughts in some places, but heavier rainfall and more flooding in others.

🌳 Many plants and animals would lose their habitats at between 1.7 and 3.6°F. Take green sea turtles, for example. If the temperature of the sand where their eggs are laid is warmer than 88°F, the baby turtles will be female. If the sand is cooler than 82°F, the babies will be male. Green turtles need both males and females to keep their species alive.

Save Our Brothers

🌳 Changed climate conditions could result in many insects losing their habitats and even going extinct. We rely on insects, like bees and butterflies, to pollinate plants that provide our food. Without them, humans and other animals could starve.

🌳 Frozen permafrost soil will melt. This is important because permafrost stores carbon, which would be released in the melting ice and will only add to the problem.

Surface temperature rises.

When it thaws, levels of CO_2 and methane in the atmosphere increase.

Active layer that thaws in the summer.

When permafrost thaws, the active layer gets deeper.

Permafrost is soil, gravel, sand, and the remains of dead plants and animals held together by ice that has been frozen for at least two years.

🌳 Levels of oxygen in the ocean will go down because of the higher concentration of CO_2 in the water, causing corals, shellfish, algae, and fish to die.

🌳 Many people will find it hard to survive the heat and many will suffer from lack of food and water, especially in poorer countries. Limiting warming to 2.7°F could prevent poverty for several hundred million people by 2050.

So it's crucial to keep the increase in temperature as low as possible. The trouble is, to hit the Paris Agreement target, emissions must start decreasing NOW and reach zero by 2070.

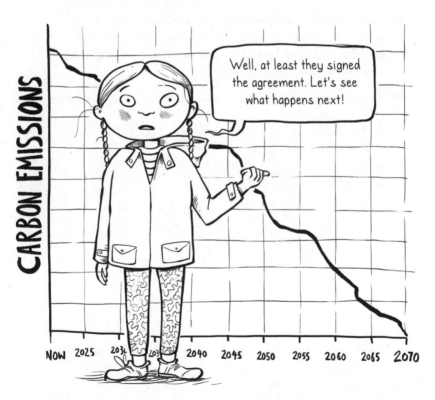

5   GRETA GOES ON STRIKE

Unfortunately, Greta was about to be bitterly disappointed.

THE NEW PRESIDENT

The Paris Agreement came into force on November 4, 2016. Five days later, on November 9, Donald Trump was declared the winner of the US election and was about to become the forty-fifth president of the United States of America. Trump had some very strong and dangerous views:

> I think climate change is a trick thought up by the Chinese to attack the US manufacturing industry.*

*This is a false and racist claim.

He'd tweeted things like:

Donald J. Trump ✓
@realDonaldTrump
It's freezing outside, where the hell is "global warming"?

Sigh. You can't work out climate change by looking at one day's weather. Look at some actual science!

He'd even claimed that climate change is:

a hoax . . . it's a moneymaking industry.

Um, no it isn't. It's some moneymaking industries that are causing the problem in the first place!

Trump was in favor of supporting coal mining and other fossil-fuel industries. He didn't care about their carbon footprint, because they brought plenty of jobs and plenty of money. His "energy experts" were people who either had links to the fossil-fuel industry or to organizations that say climate change isn't happening.

The horrible truth was that **a climate-change denier** was now the leader of the most powerful country in the world! You'd think the news would have plunged Greta back into a deep depression. Her family did worry about how she would react. But when the result was announced, Greta surprised them by saying that having a climate-change denier for US president was a good thing! It would wake people up and encourage them to act. President Trump freely admitted that he supported fossil-fuel industries and wasn't bothered about reducing greenhouse-gas emissions—while other leaders were doing as little as he was, while pretending to care about the climate crisis.

The United States is responsible for more of the excess carbon emissions that are warming the planet than any other country in the world except China. So US policies on climate change are massively important if the world's going to act effectively against climate change.

In June 2017, Trump announced that **the USA would pull out of the Paris Agreement.**

Luckily, when Joe Biden became president in 2021, he changed this right away.

WILD WEATHER

There were some devastating results of climate change in 2017. Around the world thousands of people died in flooding, landslides, and terrible hurricanes.

Then, **things got even worse**. In California in 2018, wildfires burned nearly 3,000 square miles of land. In 2019, after months of drought, fires began to spread through eastern Australia and were soon burning on a scale never seen before, destroying more than 71,800 square miles of land and nearly 6,000 buildings, including thousands of homes. At least thirty-four people and more than a billion animals were killed. Over 330 tons of CO_2 were released.

No one can definitively say that these events were directly caused by climate change, but we can definitely say that extreme weather events are becoming more and more common as a result of the warming climate. We now have four times more extreme weather events than we used to have fifty years ago.

In the summer of 2017, a group of scientists warned that we only had **three years left** to start reducing emissions of CO_2, if we were going to meet the Paris Agreement target. Missing this target could start a spiral of disaster that's completely out of our control.

Guess what? CO_2 emissions increased.

In March 2018, the United Nations Secretary-General, António Guterres, said that:

Climate change is the greatest threat facing humankind.

And STILL no one's doing anything! Aaarrghh!

GRETA DOES SOME POLAR RESEARCH

In July 2018, Greta found herself hot and **up a mountain** with Svante and Roxy the dog. They were hiking up Mount Nuolja in the far north of Sweden, while staying in the village of Abisko at the bottom of the mountain.

Abisko is home to the Swedish Polar Research Secretariat, and Greta and her dad were there to meet with professors and students and learn more about climate change in the Arctic. They'd traveled all the way in the family's electric car.

This part of Sweden is inside the Arctic Circle. Its summers are usually mild, not hot—but that's changing as the climate warms. While Greta was there, the temperature reached **a sweltering 89°F**.

We lose around 15,000 tons of Arctic ice every second!

This sea ice is critical to the survival of marine life. Narwhals, polar bears and walruses are all at risk here, while new species are moving in as the Arctic warms. Red foxes have moved further north, for example, and they're killing smaller Arctic foxes.

But melting ice also provides opportunities for humans to go where they've never been before. As the ice melts, ships are taking advantage.

With less sea ice we could knock days off a journey.

SS ICE SMASHER

Ships bring pollution and sometimes spill their cargoes. The noise they make causes problems, too.

68

Whales use sound to communicate under water, it also helps them hunt for food.
But noise from shipping is making this harder. Whales can also be killed when ships crash into them.

Ow!

There's oil and other important minerals under the Arctic, which is worth thousands of billions of dollars, and big companies are lining up to figure out how they can extract them. Donald Trump even offered to buy Greenland for its oil reserves.

Greenland is not for sale!

This is happening even though fossil fuels are a big part of the reason the Arctic is warming in the first place!

Greta and her dad discovered that warmer temperatures were **killing off the trees** on Mount Nuolja. Fifty years earlier, the treeline of the forests had started 750 feet further down the mountainside.

Beneath them, enormous freight trains rumbled past carrying iron ore, extracted from further north, to the coast to be shipped around the world. It would be used to make cars and washing machines and other goods the world's richest countries consume so much of, adding to the problem and making the temperature rise even more.

What they were witnessing was depressing, but Greta seemed a little less anxious than usual. They were hiking with four students and a member of staff from the Secretariat. At lunchtime everyone sat on the ground and ate together. Even Greta. **Svante was amazed**. It was the first time she'd eaten in front of strangers in about four years!

Inside the Polar Research Secretariat, something else astonishing happened. During one of the lectures the professor asked if anyone knew the efficiency rate of solar panels. The students shrugged, Svante racked his brains. Under the table Roxy the dog slept.

Then **Greta raised her hand** and said:

It's 16%.

It was the right answer! The professor was impressed, and so were the students. But Svante nearly fell off his chair. He wasn't surprised that Greta knew the answer. He was surprised that she'd answered at all. She hadn't willingly spoken to anyone except her immediate family and her one teacher for years.

TIME FOR ACTION!

Greta seemed to be getting better, and it might have been because a plan was starting to form in her mind. She'd been thinking about it for a long time, and she knew she had to take action. She hadn't known exactly what to do at first, so she'd done what she does best: she'd studied. And she'd discovered that small people who didn't seem to have power could change things—it had happened before. When Greta learned about an activist named Rosa Parks, she counted her as one of her heroes immediately.

GRETA'S HEROES: ROSA PARKS

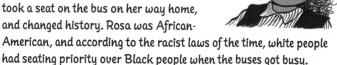

On the evening of December 1, 1955, in Montgomery, Alabama, Rosa Parks took a seat on the bus on her way home, and changed history. Rosa was African-American, and according to the racist laws of the time, white people had seating priority over Black people when the buses got busy.

When Rosa refused to give up her seat for a white passenger, she was arrested and charged a fine. She refused to pay.

The buses in Montgomery relied on Black passengers. In protest at Rosa's treatment, all Black people refused to use them—even though it meant walking miles to and from work. They kept up their boycott for 381 days until, finally, the bus company gave in. The bus law and other racist laws like it were scrapped, thanks to Rosa.

It's nice and dry in here—plenty of room in the back!

When Greta discovered that Rosa was quiet and shy, just like she was, she admired her even more! It made her realize that you don't have to be bold and outgoing to make a difference. What Rosa had done had been simple; she'd just been **brave enough to say no**.

Then there were the March for Our Lives protesters in the United States.

On February 14, 2018, a gunman had walked into Marjory Stoneman Douglas High School in Parkland, Florida, and opened fire. He killed seventeen people, many of them students. There had been many school shootings in the United States before this, and young people had had enough. Students walked out of their classes in protest, and on March 24, 2018, demonstrations took place across the United States, with **over 200,000 people marching** in Washington to demand stricter gun laws. Parkland students organized and spoke at the rally. One of them was Emma Gonzalez. Clearly angry and with tears in her eyes, she listed the names of those killed at her school and then stood in silence for four minutes and twenty-four seconds— the time it had taken the gunman to carry out his crime. Emma was just eighteen. Her speech quickly traveled around the world and made a massive impact.

Emma only joined Twitter after the attack, but it wasn't long before she'd gained over a million followers.

The march was the biggest gun control protest the United States had ever seen, it was organized by young people, and **it made a difference**—as a direct result, the state of Florida started to amend its gun laws.

The Parkland students' crisis was very different from Greta's, but that didn't mean she couldn't organize something similar in Sweden. She'd already been talking to her parents about a school strike. They weren't at all keen on the idea, and they made it clear that if she went ahead with it, she'd be doing it on her own. But that didn't stop Greta. Svante warned her that she'd have to be prepared to answer questions about everything and know her arguments inside out. Greta already did know her arguments inside out.

In May 2018, an essay Greta had written about climate change was one of the winning entries in a competition run by a Swedish newspaper. In it she'd written: *"I want to feel safe. How can I feel safe when I know we are in the greatest crisis in human history?'* Fifteen-year-old Greta had convinced the newspaper, but she didn't do so well in persuading other young people to join her in a school strike. Still, she didn't let it bother her. Greta was so determined it was the right thing to do, that, inspired by her heroes, **she decided to do the strike**—even if she had to do it alone.

SCHOOL STRIKE FOR THE CLIMATE

Schools start early after the summer vacation in Sweden, and August 20, 2018, should have been Greta's first day back. Instead, she packed her backpack with reference materials on the climate crisis and 100 flyers full of facts that she'd made herself. She grabbed her school textbooks too (she might be missing school, but that didn't mean she wouldn't do the work!) along with a lunchbox, water bottle, cushion, and jumper. Then she set off on her bicycle in the direction of the Swedish parliament building, the Riksdag.

Svante cycled anxiously behind her, balancing **a rather special piece of hardboard** under one arm. They'd bought it from a local builders' merchants and painted on a simple message:

That's Swedish for "School Strike for the Climate."

A few days before, Greta had checked out the best place to position herself, and now she locked up her bicycle, took the sign from Svante, and waved goodbye to him as she crossed the bridge to begin her strike alone.

The plan was to school strike until September 7, 2018, two days before the Swedish parliamentary elections.

At first, nothing much happened. Most people ignored Greta and carried on with their busy lives. A couple of women stopped to insist she should go back to school. She had absolutely no intention of following their advice, but she did carry on studying her school textbooks.

Up until that point, Greta had mostly used her social media accounts to post pictures of her beloved dogs, but now she boldly asked a passerby to take a photo of her with her phone and then posted it on Twitter and Instagram. **She hardly had any followers**, but she hoped that word might still spread.

And it did! Thanks to a few influential family friends. First the climate campaigner Staffan Lindberg retweeted Greta's post. Then the weather expert Pär Holmgren followed suit, along with singer-songwriter Stefan Sundström. Between them they had more than 30,000 followers. Greta's social media posts began to go viral.

A documentary film crew had found out what Greta was planning, and they turned up to ask if they could film the strike. Greta said OK. Next came a photographer, then the newspaper reporters. Greta couldn't believe things were happening so quickly, but the girl who not so long ago would barely speak managed to answer the reporters' questions clearly and calmly. It was scary, of course, but Greta knew that if she didn't talk to the reporters it would stop her from achieving her goals. She faced her fears every single day, and soon they stopped bothering her as much.

After 3 p.m., at the end of the school day, she cycled home with Svante. He could tell just by looking at her that **she felt genuinely happy**. It was only her first day of action, but it was already making a big difference to Greta.

On the second day, a year-nine student named Mayson sat down to strike beside Greta.

That was a big step, from one to two.

From that moment on, she was never alone. Greta kept up with her schoolwork the whole time, and only posted one image on her phone each day, because in school she wouldn't have been allowed to use it. The numbers of strikers continued to grow and grow . . .

On the third day of the strike, Greta tweeted that "almost 35 people!" were striking with her. Two people arrived from Greenpeace (an organization that's been campaigning to protect the environment for over fifty years) and offered their support—and **a tub of vegan noodles**. Svante and Malena were worried that Greta hadn't been eating enough while she was striking because she'd been too distracted. But when Svante saw Greta accepting the noodles without question and eating the whole tub, he knew the school strike was having a magical effect on his daughter.

Every day, more people joined in.

Until, on September 7, the last day of the strike, more than 1,000 people were protesting alongside her.

After a couple of weeks of the strike, when a major foreign-language newspaper wanted to interview Greta, **she handled it wonderfully**. The small, anxious fifteen-year-old was becoming world-famous and finding her voice at last.

6   GRETA'S REBELLION

On September 8, 2018, the day after the school strike ended, tens of thousands of people were taking part in marches around the world to demand action on climate change, and Greta had decided to join the People's Climate March in Stockholm. She was planning to do something way outside her comfort zone, something her parents would hardly have believed possible.

Before the march started, **2,000 people had gathered in the park**, and more were on their way—far more than usual for this sort of event. Some of them were demonstrating for the very first time. Maybe they'd been inspired by Greta's school strike?

As Svante watched, terrified, from the side, worrying that his daughter might run away, or burst into tears, Greta stepped onto the open-air platform with three of her fellow strikers. She knew the power of the spoken word, and she was about to use it to make a speech in front of the enormous crowd.

TV cameras rolled in and microphones were set up. At first Greta spoke in Swedish, asking everyone to take out their phones and film the speech she was about to make, so they could share it on social media.

Switching to English, to make sure that more people around the world would understand her, she introduced three other schoolstrikers and explained that they had been striking for the last three weeks and that they planned to continue the school strike every Friday.

They weren't going to make specific demands, but they would carry on until Sweden was in line with the Paris Agreement. Greta urged people all over the world to join in by protesting outside their own parliament buildings.

The grown-ups have failed us . . . We must take action into our own hands, starting today. Everyone is welcome. Everyone is needed. Please join in.

Greta finished speaking, and as **the crowd whooped, clapped, and cheered**, someone asked Svante whether he was proud. Svante said it wasn't pride he was feeling, he was *"just so endlessly happy because I can see that she's feeling good."*

Fridays for Future

The school strike had been a massive success, far better than Greta could have hoped for even in her wildest dreams. But she knew she had to keep spreading the message. Climate scientists had been issuing dire predictions for decades, but most people still didn't understand the extent of the crisis, largely because of the lack of attention in the newspapers. And people didn't want to believe the situation was really bad. It was difficult and upsetting to face the facts, and if someone told them not to worry about it, most people would happily do just that.

The world was still in a desperate crisis, but Greta had realized something astonishing:

No one is too small to make a difference.

Greta went to school again the following Monday, but she was back in front of the parliament building on Friday. **And she'd been busy**. After posting a short video on Instagram, explaining why she was striking, the hashtags #FridaysForFuture and #ClimateStrike had quickly spread. Soon, children and adults were striking in other parts of Europe, and then other parts of the world.

And we're not stopping until real action is taken to reduce our carbon emissions to net zero!

NET ZERO, EXPLAINED

"Net zero" means not adding any further greenhouse gases to the atmosphere, and it's our ultimate goal if we're going to halt global warming.

There are two countries in the world that have already achieved national net zero—Suriname in South America and Bhutan in South Asia. They've managed it because they are small countries that don't produce many goods, because they have a lot of forest to absorb the carbon, and by getting their energy from hydroelectricity.

hydroelectric dam

In 2019 the UK and France became the first countries with big economies to pass laws saying when they planned to achieve net zero. They both say they're aiming for **2050**. The UK and France set a trend, and soon other countries began pledging to reduce emissions. Most are aiming for net zero by **2050**, but Sweden has pledged **2045**, Finland is aiming for **2035**, and Uruguay an impressive **2030**.

Some companies are making plans to become net zero too.

But there's no point in countries saying they're going to reach net zero in thirty years, if they don't DO something to start reducing emissions right away.

For countries to achieve net zero by **2050** and for the world to achieve the Paris Agreement warming target, they would need to start reducing emissions immediately by at least **15%**. And that doesn't seem to be happening so far.

For the whole world to become net zero, it's going to mean huge changes.

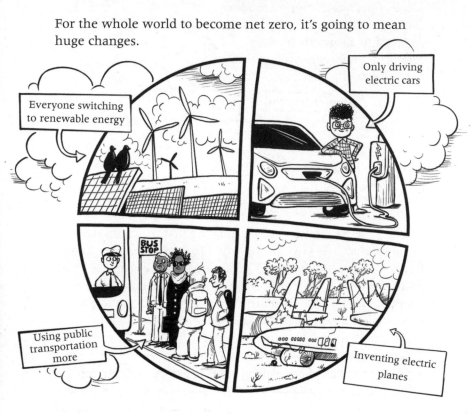

Everyone switching to renewable energy

Only driving electric cars

Using public transportation more

Inventing electric planes

We need to develop new ways of doing things. They might include:

🌳 Building smart homes, designed to use far less energy.

🌳 Building smart roads that charge up your electric car as you drive it.

🌳 Planting millions of trees.

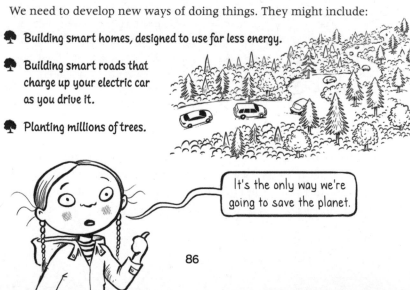

It's the only way we're going to save the planet.

EXTINCTION REBELLION

Greta wasn't the only one trying to find new ways to take action on the climate crisis. In May 2018, a new organization called Extinction Rebellion (XR for short) was founded in the United Kingdom.

Like Greta, XR wanted to draw attention to the climate crisis and the environment, and some of its members weren't afraid to break the law to make their point (though they were completely against any use of violence). XR's aim is to get governments to declare a climate and ecological emergency, and to reduce carbon emissions to net zero. Greta thought XR was absolutely great, and when she heard that the group planned to occupy a space in front of the British Houses of Parliament in London and make a "Declaration of Rebellion," **she just couldn't stay away**.

The Declaration of Rebellion was being planned for the end of October, not long after Greta's school strike. News of the strike had spread and, of course, XR thought that Greta was absolutely great too, so they invited her to come and make a speech. This was an opportunity she definitely didn't want to miss.

Less than two months after her first speech at the end of her school strike, she and her dad arrived in London in time for Halloween 2018.

Greta looked tiny as she addressed the crowd. Sirens wailed behind her, and traffic noise threatened to drown out her quiet voice. So she spoke each line and then paused for everyone who could hear her to repeat what she'd said. That way the whole audience got to hear her words. She talked about being in the middle of a sixth mass extinction.

THE SIXTH MASS EXTINCTION, EXPLAINED

This is the extinction XR wants to rebel against.

The five mass extinctions that have happened in the history of Planet Earth all took place millions of years ago, long before human beings existed. One of them wiped out the dinosaurs.

Scientists now say we're experiencing a sixth mass extinction, and humans are to blame—climate change, loss of habitat, pollution, and hunting are causing many animal species to die out completely.

This planet is home to the only living things we know about in the universe. We depend on the world's plants and animals for food, to pollinate plants, to keep the soil healthy, to help maintain the climate, and hundreds of other things.

Here are just a few animals that are in danger of extinction:

RED PANDA

SUMATRAN ORANGUTAN

WRINKLED HORNBILL

Yet we're in the process of causing thousands of them to die out completely every year.

There are 200 species going extinct every single day.

Extinction is a natural process, but the rates it's happening at today are about 1,000 times higher than they should be.

A quarter of all mammals are threatened with extinction. Insect populations are declining dramatically. One day, even human beings could die out!

London's Natural History Museum was so impressed by Greta's campaign against climate change that they named a tiny beetle *Nelloptodes gretae* in her honor in 2019.

Undiscovered insects are going extinct all the time, before we even have a chance to name them.

ENTOMOLOGIST

Nelloptodes gretae

More Extinction Rebellion protests happened in London over the following months, and protesters certainly got themselves noticed. In their aim to cause disruption they glued themselves to trains, blocked roads, and protested outside oil company headquarters and at Heathrow, London's biggest airport, which had plans for expansion. At one point, they brought Oxford Circus, part of London's famous shopping district, to a standstill. Shoppers, cars, and buses found **a pink boat** in the way! It stayed there for five days, until the police managed to take it away.

Hundreds of protesters were arrested. When Greta got a chance to speak to the UK parliament, she criticized the UK's use of fossil fuels and its plans to expand airports. She and lots of other protesters were very happy when the expansion plans were eventually dropped.

7   GRETA GOES GLOBAL

Only a few weeks had passed since Greta had first sat alone outside the Swedish parliament building, but she'd become world-famous. Every time she spoke, her message was carried around the world via news articles and social media. She'd often complained to her mom—who was, of course, a famous singer—that no celebrities were standing up against the climate crisis.

But now Greta couldn't complain as much anymore, because **she'd become a celebrity** herself.

I really wasn't expecting that.

CLIMATE CHANGE IN KATOWICE

After that first Extinction Rebellion speech, Greta was in high demand. In December 2018, there was a Climate Change Conference (COP24) in Katowice, Poland, organized by the United Nations. Greta was on her way, with her dad at the wheel of their little electric car. It took them two days to make the trip to Poland, but neither of them doubted that it would be worth it.

Plenty of people are terrified of speaking in public. There's even a word for it: glossophobia. But it doesn't bother Greta at all. Even when she was faced with a conference room full of dark-suited delegates from around the world at COP24, **she wasn't nervous**—she wanted to make sure she got her point across, but she didn't worry about how she looked or sounded. She stepped up to the podium to make her speech, addressing the Secretary General of the United Nations, António Guterres.

We need to keep the fossil fuels in the ground, and we need to focus on equity . . . We have run out of excuses and we are running out of time. We have come here to let you know that change is coming, whether you like it or not. The real power belongs to the people.

COP24 KATOWICE
POLAND 2018

CLIMATE JUSTICE, EXPLAINED

"Equity" basically means fairness. Quite simply, right now, the richer you are, the more emissions you're responsible for.

The richest 10% of people in the world are creating half of the greenhouse gases that are in our atmosphere because of human activity.

The poorest 50% of people are responsible for less than 10% of those gases.

The people who have contributed the least to the climate change crisis are going to suffer the most, which is obviously completely unfair.

Climate justice is all about admitting that this is true and getting rich countries to aim for net zero carbon emissions faster than poorer countries, even if it means poorer countries have to continue using fossil fuels for some time.

The conference at Katowice went on for two weeks, and while it was great that Greta's speech was shared with millions around the world, it wasn't so great that the US delegates were trying to throw a wrench in the works. President Trump's energy adviser said that countries had a right to use their own natural resources and that the United States would carry on digging up its fossil fuels. When protesters drowned him out with cries of "Shame on you!" and "Keep it in the ground!," **Greta couldn't help smiling**.

On social media, she appealed for people to join her in the following Friday's climate strike. Then she and Svante hurried back to Sweden in time to take part.

GRETA IN SWITZERLAND

Early in the new year, Greta and Svante headed to Davos, a small town in Switzerland with an enormous ski resort. Every year since 1971, it's hosted the World Economic Forum (WEF), which brings people together to try to find ways to improve the world. Some of the most important politicians, businesspeople, scientists, and artists on the planet attend the forum, but it's strictly invitation only. Amazingly, Greta, the small, quiet, now just sixteen-year-old girl who'd refused to eat and been bullied at school, received an invitation to the 2019 forum. She was determined to get there—even after she discovered it would involve **a thirty-two-hour train ride** each way!

Greta and her dad stepped from the train into the January snow and were greeted by a forest of microphones. Greta answered the reporters' questions politely, then she and Svante went to find where they were staying.

While some conference delegates swooped in on their own (fossil-fuel-guzzling) private jets and booked luxury rooms that cost thousands of dollars, Greta's accommodation looked like this:

Greta hadn't just committed to the carbon-conserving train journey; she was keeping her carbon footprint super low—by **staying in a tent**!

A team of scientists had set up an Arctic Basecamp at Davos, using actual expedition tents. They planned to work in the camp during the day, and sleep there at night. They wanted to remind WEF delegates about the melting ice at the poles.

Greta posted smiling pictures on social media as she climbed into her sleeping bag.

It's quite cozy, really!

But at night, temperature could drop as low as -0.4°F! So it's not surprising she kept her hat and scarf on.

Greta wasn't the only celebrity at Davos and she met Bono and will.i.am, who were there to take part in a panel discussion. But far more exciting was getting a chance to speak with one of her all-time heroes: scientist and conservationist, Jane Goodall.

GRETA'S HEROES: JANE GOODALL

In 1960, when she was twenty-six, Jane Goodall moved from England to East Africa to study chimpanzees, human beings' closest living relatives, in the wild. She became the world's top expert on these fascinating creatures, and is still working to protect their habitat and save them from extinction. She gives speeches on the threats faced by chimpanzees and the people who live close to them, as well as other environmental issues. She is also committed to protecting Planet Earth, so it's not surprising that Greta admires her so much.

And you give me hope for the future.

PLAIN SPEAKING

Greta gave her speech at Davos on January 25. She spoke calmly about the **terrible disaster** that was unfolding while most people were just carrying on as normal.

Greta was saying that the whole world was a home for all people. And if your home is on fire, you don't just sit around pretending it isn't happening. You get up and do something about it.

In her speech she blamed the rich and leaders of huge companies for the climate crisis. Some of them were at the Davos meeting, and she wasn't afraid to call them out.

Some people, some companies, some decision makers in particular know exactly what priceless values they have been sacrificing to continue making unimaginable amounts of money, and I think many of you here today belong to that group of people.

You have to be brave to stand up in front of some of the world's most influential people and say that sort of thing. Greta was talking about fossil-fuel companies and other companies that contribute to greenhouse-gas emissions—the people who run those companies get very rich, at the expense of Planet Earth. There were **so many extremely wealthy people** in the room as she spoke that Greta's words were bound to apply to some of them. She wanted to tell the truth, and if it made some of her audience feel uncomfortable, well, good! Maybe they'd think more about their actions in future.

Some speakers on climate change try to sound optimistic and focus on the positive, but not Greta. She thinks **too much optimism is part of the problem**—it allows people to tell themselves everything's OK, and if they think everything's OK, they don't bother to act. She wasn't impressed by most of the famous people at Davos, or the serious, important-looking ones in suits. She might have been impressed if there'd been an agreement to take action on the climate crisis—proper steps to ending the use of fossil fuels. But, sadly, no such agreement happened.

A few weeks later, at the European Economic and Social Committee in Brussels, Greta gave another group of grown-ups a good talking to.

Greta's speeches are really powerful, so you could be forgiven for thinking she must have someone writing them for her. But that's not the case.

Books, Music, and More Speeches

Greta's direct way of speaking has certainly got her noticed. In January 2018 she had been invited to give a TED talk. TED stands for Technology, Entertainment, Design and is a non-profit organization that wants to spread ideas on all sorts of things—science, architecture, business, art, just about any subject you could name.

The ideas are usually presented as short talks by people the organization considers to be outstanding thinkers. At sixteen years old, Greta was one of the youngest people to be asked. Her talk explained why she had started her school strike, and urged everyone to take action. **It's been viewed over five million times.**

In May 2019, some of her speeches were published in a book called *No One Is Too Small to Make a Difference*. Greta won the 2019 Waterstones Author of the Year Award for it in the UK.

Generally, Malena and Beata are the musical ones of the family, but early in 2019 Greta had got involved in music too. Award-winning band The 1975 were worried about the climate crisis, and they wanted to say something about it with their music. Who better to ask for lyrics than Greta? She wrote them an essay and the band traveled to Sweden to record her speaking the words she'd written to a background of music the band had written. The recording features on The 1975's album *Notes on a Conditional Form*. It was set to release in 2020, but the band felt Greta's track, also called "The 1975," was too important to wait that long, so they brought it out in July 2019. All proceeds from the recording went to Extinction Rebellion, as Greta had asked.

As if book publishing, music recording, and studying her school subjects weren't enough, Greta was also busy with other things early in 2019.

She traveled to Italy to meet Pope Francis, the head of the Catholic Church, who agrees with her on the climate crisis. The Pope holds "audiences" where he speaks to a big crowd of people in St. Peter's Square in Rome, and Greta sat in the front row so that she could thank him for speaking about climate change. Pope Francis is, of course, also a fan of Greta's, and told her to carry on the good work.

She spoke at a film and television awards ceremony in Berlin, Germany, and at the Houses of Parliament in London, England. Each new event meant more publicity for the school strike, and soon **more than a million people in over 125 countries** were taking part in Fridays For Future.

All this was happening before Greta had officially finished school!

8   Greta's North American Adventure

In June 2019, Greta left school with fourteen A and three B grades. She figured she might have gotten straight As if it hadn't been for the school strikes.

In Sweden, school isn't required after you're sixteen. Greta wasn't ready to give up on her education, but she thought it might be a good idea to take a year off. She'd had another invitation from the United Nations to speak at their Climate Action Summit that September . . . in New York! **Greta really wanted to be there**.

The plan was to go to New York, then travel around North America before driving down to Santiago, Chile, where the 2019 United Nations Climate Change Conference (COP25) was scheduled to happen in December. Whether he liked it or not, Svante would be going too.

But how on earth were they going to get there? Traveling by train or electric car was obviously not an option, thanks to the inconvenient location of the Atlantic Ocean. Flying was definitely not an option either. Greta thought about hitching a ride on a container ship. But a much better solution turned up in the extraordinary form of an actual prince, who offered Greta and Svante the use of his **solar-powered yacht**. Prince Pierre Casiraghi of Monaco was also offering his own services—he was planning on skippering the boat himself, along with professional sailor Boris Herrmann.

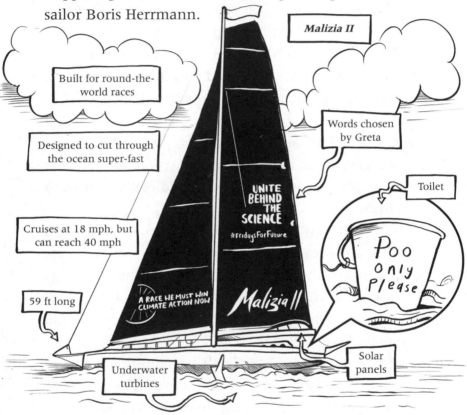

Malizia II

Built for round-the-world races

Words chosen by Greta

Designed to cut through the ocean super-fast

UNITE BEHIND THE SCIENCE
#FridaysForFuture

Toilet

Cruises at 18 mph, but can reach 40 mph

A RACE WE MUST WIN CLIMATE ACTION NOW

Malizia II

Poo Only Please

59 ft long

Underwater turbines

Solar panels

The *Malizia II* is an around-the-world racing yacht. Sails propel the boat with the help of the wind, then solar panels and underwater turbines provide electricity for lighting, the radio, and other equipment. It was like being able to walk to New York, since the trip was **completely emission-free**. The yacht was designed for speed rather than comfort. It had four bunk beds, but no kitchen, shower or, er, toilet! But what it lacks in facilities it makes up for in cutting-edge navigation equipment. There's actually an on-board science lab!

Greta and Svante began driving all the way from Sweden to England in early August, before sailing from Plymouth on the south-west coast—the same place the *Mayflower* had sailed from nearly 400 years earlier, taking the first European settlers to America.

Setting off on August 14, Greta had books and board games to keep her busy during the journey, and a toy rabbit—a gift from a friend—to make up for not having Moses and Roxy to cuddle. Meals were freeze-dried packets of vegan food mixed with water and heated on a small stove. They were cut off from the rest of the world (except when they used the satellite phone), but Greta didn't mind that, or the conditions on board. She saw dolphins and other sea creatures and on clear nights **she loved gazing up at the stars**.

It was **a grueling fifteen days**, but thankfully she didn't get seasick, and on the afternoon of August 28, Greta approached her destination to a hero's reception. Crowds had waited for hours to catch a glimpse of her. As the yacht skirted round the Statue of Liberty, a flotilla of seventeen United Nations sailing boats appeared to escort *Malizia* in to New York harbor. Each boat had one of the UN's sustainable development goals for 2030 emblazoned on its sails, from vaccinating children against disease to cutting down on plastics.

Sailing the Atlantic was an incredible experience. But underneath the yacht, the seas were in terrible trouble.

ACIDIC OCEANS

> Most excess CO_2 stays in the atmosphere, trapping heat and warming the planet. But about a third of it is absorbed by the oceans, making them more acidic.

Life on Earth is in such a delicate balance that this "acidification" has a big effect:

🌳 Weakening coral reefs, which are home to 25% of all sea life, even though they take up less than 2% of the sea floor.

🌳 Affecting plant life, fish, and all creatures that live in the water.

Acid weakens creatures with shells.

Less food for the creatures that eat them.

🌳 Creating "dead zones" where hardly any life can exist.

PLASTIC SEAS

> Remember the floating plastic trash pile island from page 1? It's there because humans are constantly throwing away plastic without thinking about where it will end up.

🌳 A truckload of plastic finds its way into the world's oceans every single minute! And it gets everywhere: from deep-sea trenches to desert island beaches.

🌳 Plastic breaks down into tiny particles that don't go away.

🌳 Some plastic particles, called microbeads, find their way into the sea because they can't be filtered out of waste water. They can come from washing clothes made from artificial materials and they're even in some make-up and toothpastes!

🌳 Sea creatures can be injured or trapped by bigger pieces of plastic. Sometimes they mistake it for food.

Jellyfish, yum!

There's another threat to our seas: companies want to mine the minerals and metals on the ocean floor. The scaly-foot snail was the first species to be listed as threatened because of deep-sea mining. But it's unlikely to be the last:

WHAT YOU CAN DO: You can help to stop the problem from getting worse by doing your best not to buy anything in the sort of plastic packaging that can only be used once. Avoid using plastic straws and carry your own reusable water bottle with you when you can.

GRETA MEETS A PRESIDENT

Setting foot on dry land was a bit of a shock for Greta after being on the ocean for so long. Her legs felt wobbly, and she wasn't quite prepared for the noise and the smell of the city. But after a couple of days' rest, it was **back to business**. As it was a Friday, the most important thing to do was to climate strike—this time outside the United Nations building, a skyscraper in the middle of New York City.

Greta then took a trip to Washington, D.C. to meet a president—but not the climate-change-denying President Trump. Instead she met his predecessor, the forty-fourth president of the United States, Barack Obama. He is concerned about the environment and had put climate policies in place while he was president. Unfortunately, President Trump was busy reversing them. Barack Obama is yet another of Greta's fans, and he's called her:

One of our planet's greatest advocates.

Greta certainly had her work cut out spreading the message about the climate crisis in the United States. On average around 3% of the world's population are climate-change deniers, but in the United States it's as many as **12% of people**—including the country's president in 2019. So Greta was happy and relieved that plenty of American people felt moved enough to act with her. Hundreds of other young climate strikers joined her in Washington for a protest, then marched with her to the White House.

At the United States Congress in Washington, Greta gave a speech and took part in a discussion. That same day, the Trump administration was busy **trying to stop** the state of California bringing in new laws that would limit emissions from cars and trucks.

What to Say to a Climate-Change Denier
(or to anyone who thinks climate change isn't that serious)

Greta has some good responses to climate deniers' claims.

And I don't mind if you use them too.

"It won't be that bad—we'll all learn to adapt."

It is that bad. You only need to look at pages 28 and 29 to realize that. People will end up without food and homes, thousands of plant and animal species could go extinct, maybe even humans.

"It'll only affect people far away. It won't bother us in our rich country."

Oh yes it will! Cities and coastal areas all over the world will be flooded as sea levels rise. All countries will be affected by migration, as people lose their homes, and by food and water shortages.

"Me giving up flying or meat is hardly going to make a difference."

I agree that companies and governments are the ones that really need to change. But there are an awful lot of individuals in the world, and if millions of us change our lifestyles and stand up for the climate it definitely will make a difference.

"It's too depressing. It's better to ignore climate change and just enjoy life."

Well, the future doesn't have to be terrible—not if we do something about it.

"Hasn't Earth's climate always changed over time, naturally?"

Yes, long ago parts of the world that are warm today used to be covered in ice. BUT over the last 200 years climate change has been huge and rapid and there's no doubt that it's happening because of human activity.

"The real problem is that the world population is too big."

Our emissions are the real problem: the richer you are, the greater your emissions (see page 95). If we stop emitting greenhouse gases, we can- solve the problem without having to reduce the population of the world.

"New inventions and technology will solve the crisis."

Scientists are working on carbon-capture technology, to suck CO_2 out of the atmosphere, but it doesn't exist yet, so we really can't count on it. There are no electric planes operating yet, either—only prototypes. We hope to have these things soon, but they won't be invented or developed fast enough. We need to start reducing carbon emissions now.

3

"I can offset my carbon emissions so I don't need to worry about eating steak and flying around the world."

To balance out their carbon footprints, individuals and companies can give money to environmental projects. So, for every flight they take, they might pay to have some trees planted. But ideally they should be paying for the trees as well as giving up steaks and flying.

My mom says carbon offsetting is a bit like getting someone in a poor country to go on a diet for you. It makes us think we don't have to bother doing anything ourselves.

How Dare You?

Greta was back in New York in plenty of time for the United Nations Summit. It was just over a year since her first strike in Stockholm, when she sat outside the Swedish parliament building all by herself. Things had changed quite a bit since then! Plans were underway for the biggest school strike yet, and on Friday September 20, 2019, four million children and workers (invited to join in for the first time) took action in 150 countries around the world.

About 250,000 people joined Greta in New York. This wasn't just the biggest school strike ever, it was the biggest climate protest ever. And it was still going on as Greta climbed into bed at the end of her day, because protesting crowds were still marching on the other side of the world, in Melbourne, Australia, in the warmth of the afternoon sun.

Greta Thunberg
@GretaThunberg

The summit opened the following Monday. After making such a huge effort to get there, **Greta was ready.** In her speech, she expressed how furious she was at the lack of action on the climate crisis.

How dare you pretend that this can be solved with just "business as usual" and some technical solutions? . . . You are failing us. But the young people are starting to understand your betrayal. The eyes of all future generations are upon you. And if you choose to fail us, I say: we will never forgive you.

She looked angry. Really, really angry. As Greta says, there's no point in being polite when your house is on fire. Different countries announced their plans to the summit, but none of it sounded as though it was going to make a real difference to greenhouse-gas emissions. Angela Merkel, the German chancellor, promised that Germany would stop mining coal by 2038.

That is too late!

Brazil's president, Jair Bolsinaro, didn't bother going to the summit at all. And President Trump mainly popped in to see the speech by Indian prime minister, Narendra Modi. He practically brushed past Greta at one point. **She glared at him.**

HOLLYWOOD GETS THE GRETA EFFECT

Greta loved meeting Barack Obama, but she'd come to realize that many of the politicians she met only said what sounded good—it didn't mean they were going to do anything. She much preferred talking to other young activists, who were giving up their time to campaign for a better future and REALLY meant what they said. She also liked meeting some of her famous fans:

🌳 Greta went on a bike ride with her friend, environmentalist, body-building film star, and the former governor of California, Arnold Schwarzenegger (he's from Austria originally, and they'd been interviewed together in Austria earlier in the year). He even arranged an electric car for the next leg of her and Svante's journey— a Tesla Model 3, no less!

🌳 In Los Angeles, Greta met the actor and climate activist Leonardo DiCaprio, who said it was an honor to spend time with her. He posted a photo of the two of them on Instagram and less than a day later it had four million likes!

🌳 She appeared on the *Ellen DeGeneres Show*, which has an audience of millions. Ellen gave a copy of Greta's book to every member of the studio audience. She also asked an interesting question:

The actor Jane Fonda was disappointed she didn't get to meet Greta. Jane has been protesting all her life about all sorts of different things, but it was only after seeing Greta and her climate strike that she started campaigning about the climate crisis. She began protesting on Fridays and has been **arrested several times** as a result. She very nearly spent her eighty-second birthday in jail!

Driving north in the Tesla, Greta and Svante's adventure was taking them to Canada and the Jasper National Park. They struggled through a blizzard to trek across a glacier—one that probably won't be around for much longer, because of the climate crisis.

Greta had also accepted a special invitation from the tribal leaders at Standing Rock in North Dakota.

Tokata Iron Eyes was only twelve in 2016 when she first made a video calling for help for her people, the Lakota. They were battling against a proposed pipeline that would carry 570,000 barrels of crude oil past their land each day, which would pollute their drinking water and damage their land. Greta thought Tokata was **absolutely brilliant** and the two of them gave a speech together. Tokata's people must have liked Greta too, because they honored her with a Lakota name, Maphiyata echiyatan hin win, which means "woman who came from the heavens."

BACK ACROSS THE ATLANTIC

Greta had been expecting to travel down to Santiago in Chile for the COP25 Climate Change Conference, but she was in for a surprise. Because of violent political demonstrations in Chile, **the conference was suddenly moved** all the way across the ocean to

Madrid in Spain. Greta found herself on the wrong side of the Atlantic again!

She had to change her plans quickly, and decided to use the power of social media. On November 1, with the conference just over a month away, she made an appeal via Twitter to find a carbon-neutral way of getting back to Europe.

Greta's saviors were an Australian couple, Riley Whitelum and Elayna Carausu (and their baby, Lennon), who were sailing round the world. They planned to cross the Atlantic in their catamaran, *La Vagabonde*, with the help of professional sailor Nikki Henderson. This time, Greta and her dad were living in luxury, because they had cooking facilities, a shower, and even a toilet.

Aboard La Vagabonde

Unfortunately, they were crossing from Virginia to Lisbon, Portugal, at a bad time of year. Journeys across the Atlantic from west to east usually happen in May or June because the sea is calmer, there are fewer storms, and the wind is more likely to be blowing in the right direction. Traveling back to Europe was a much more challenging trip than the one that had brought them to New York. **Waves up to sixteen feet** high battered the yacht, and lightning storms crackled across the sky. No wonder Greta was seasick this time.

When she wasn't feeling seasick, Greta spent her time:

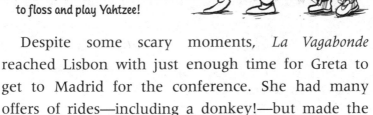

- Helping out with the meals—which included plenty of tinned soup, beans, and veggie sausages.

- Entertaining baby Lenny.

- Reading and listening to audiobooks.

- Teaching Nikki how to floss and play Yahtzee!

Despite some scary moments, *La Vagabonde* reached Lisbon with just enough time for Greta to get to Madrid for the conference. She had many offers of rides—including a donkey!—but made the last leg of her journey by train, carrying her trusty, well-traveled sign. After three weeks of floating across the ocean with just five other people for company, Greta joined a crowd of **500,000 people** demonstrating on the streets of Madrid!

When Greta spoke at COP25, she focused on how countries' promises to reduce emissions were actually misleading. They were hiding the fact that business was carrying on as normal, and the drastic changes that needed to happen weren't happening at all. People needed to put pressure on governments to make them act.

> The people who have been unaware are now starting to wake up, and once we become aware we change. We can change. People are ready for change.

THE GRETA EFFECT

As Greta had figured out, levels of greenhouse gases hadn't fallen at all. In fact, they'd risen by 4% in just four years! Greta had promised to keep protesting until countries were in line with the Paris Agreement, and **she was determined not to give up**.

The rising level of greenhouse-gas emissions

was hugely disappointing, but she was still making a difference. By March 2020 there were **13 million Fridays For Future strikers in 7,500 cities** across the world. There's even a name for the difference she's making by influencing how people live: the Greta Effect. As well as the incredible increase in climate change protests and protesters since Greta's school strike, there have been many more . . .

- Articles in newspapers, magazines, and online about the climate crisis.

- Social media posts about the climate, especially from young people.

- People taking the train instead of flying.

- People choosing to become vegetarian and vegan.

- People and companies are looking for ways to reduce their carbon emissions or "offset" them by giving money to plant trees or investing in renewable energy.

Greta has always encouraged people to vote, and in September 2019, it seems she really did have an impact. Two days after a climate strike where Greta had rallied two million protesters around the world, there was an election in Austria and the Green Party **tripled their vote**. Politicians credited Greta for motivating people to get to the polling stations.

There's still a long way to go, but other positive steps are being made. For example, China, one of the world's worst polluters, has 45% of the world's electric cars and 99% of its electric buses.

OTHER CLIMATE ACTIVISTS

More good news is that there are **lots of other activists like Greta** all over the world campaigning for climate change. There have been young people fighting ever since Severn Cullis-Suzuki made her speech back in 1992, and now, with Greta's fame and the rise of social media, these activists have a bigger platform than ever.

Come and meet some of the world's other young activists.

Howey Ou was sixteen years old when she staged China's first school strike for the climate in May 2019. Following Greta's example, she sat outside the people's government building in the city of Guilin, China. Greta has called her "a true hero."

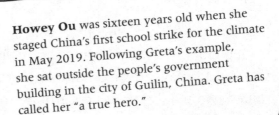

Isra Hirsi started to act on climate change when she saw oil pipelines built in Minnesota. At sixteen years old she co-founded the US Youth Climate Strike, a US branch of Greta's international movement.

Kaluki Paul Mutuku founded Green Treasures Farms in Kenya, where global warming has caused water shortages, forcing people (mainly women) to walk long distances to fetch water. His organization works with young people and women, to farm sustainably while looking after the environment.

Nina Gualinga is from the Amazon Rainforest in Ecuador and has been campaigning to protect the Amazon and about the climate crisis since she was eight years old.

Amelia Telford lives in Australia. She was nineteen when she raised money to found the Seed Indigenous Youth Climate Network, which supports young Aboriginal climate change activists to protect their culture and their land from fossil-fuel extraction and climate change.

Ridhima Pandey was only nine years old in 2017 when she tried to take the Indian government to court because it wasn't taking action on climate change. Her family had lost their homes to flooding in Uttarakhand, northern India, and over 5,500 people had died.

So many other young people are just as frustrated as I am.

TROLLS

Greta now has friends all over the world. At the start of her strike, she only had a handful of Twitter followers. Now she has **over five million**! But you don't become that famous without attracting some negative attention as well.

Greta had experience with bullies at her first school, but today's bullies mostly hide behind their computer screens. Greta finds the online trolls easier to handle than the school bullies—for a start, she doesn't have to meet them in real life. She can also see what's behind their mean social media posts; these are people who don't understand that climate change is a real thing. And making nasty comments about her proves they don't have any actual arguments.

Some of them claim she's a paid actress, others that she's making lots of money out of her campaigns.

That is completely untrue! Many of the comments are too rude to put in print!

Greta says having a famous mother has helped her cope with the trolls.

She's also learned how to write a good comeback tweet. When *Time* named Greta "Person of the Year" in 2019, President Trump wasn't happy. He'd been nominated for the same award, and he just couldn't bring himself to congratulate Greta. Instead, he tweeted:

President Trump
@realDonaldTrump

So ridiculous. Greta must work on her Anger Management problem, then go to a good old-fashioned movie with a friend! Chill, Greta, Chill!

Greta calmly responded by updating her Twitter bio:

Greta
@GretaThunberg

A teenager working on her anger management problem. Currently chilling and watching a good old-fashioned movie with a friend.

And at the end of Trump's presidency in January 2021, Greta tweeted:

Greta
@GretaThunberg

He seems like a very happy old man looking forward to a bright and wonderful future. So nice to see!

Donald Trump was **banned from Twitter** in the same month. The new US president, Joe Biden, promised to rejoin the Paris Agreement on his first day in office.

9   GRETA'S FUTURE PLANS

Greta is *Time*'s **youngest ever** Person of the Year in the whole of the magazine's ninety-two-year history. She was chosen because she had managed to do what no other scientists, researchers, or activists had been able to do: she'd got people and governments to take more notice of climate change than ever before.

At the end of a very eventful year, Greta had the honor of editing a BBC news program scheduled for the Christmas-holiday period in Britain. At the top of her list of interviewees was ninety-three-year-old naturalist and TV presenter, Sir David Attenborough. He'd been making nature documentaries since the 1950s, but his latest work, *Blue Planet II*, had shocked its viewers by showing exactly what damage plastic was doing in the oceans. Greta only met him via Skype, but it was **a great moment** for both of them:

You have aroused the world . . . I'm very grateful to you. We all are.

It was nature documentaries that first made me want to take action.

In February 2020, Greta met another one of her heroes. She was in the UK on her way to join climate strikers in Bristol and made a stop in Oxford. Not many teenagers can boast that they've been nominated for the Nobel Peace Prize, but Greta Thunberg and Malala Yousafzai had **both been nominated twice** as teenagers (though not at the same time). Malala was the youngest person ever to win the prize, when she was seventeen, and Greta had been nominated for the 2019 award and the 2020 award, also at the age of seventeen.

GRETA'S HEROES: MALALA YOUSAFZAI

When she was only eleven, Malala was well known for speaking out about education for girls in her home country, Pakistan.

I truly believe the only way we can create global peace is through not only educating our minds, but our hearts and our souls.

The extremist Taliban regime was in charge of Malala's home town, and stopped girls from going to school.

In October 2012, at the age of fifteen, Malala and two other girls were shot by a Taliban gunman on their bus home from school because the Taliban felt threatened by Malala's campaigns. Malala was shot in the head, but recovered after she was flown for treatment at a hospital in the UK, where she now lives.

The girls have at least a couple of things in common—they have **passionate beliefs** and they became famous because of them at a young age. Greta sees Malala as a role model and, after they'd met, Malala posted a picture of them both on Twitter, saying: *"She's the only friend I'd skip school for!"*

Honestly, I spend all my time encouraging kids to go to school . . .

Corona Crisis

Support for Fridays For Future was getting stronger all the time, but then things were brought to a sudden halt. At the beginning of 2020, an outbreak of a new and **deadly virus** began to spread around the world.

In March 2020, after travelling around central Europe, Greta and Svante had both fallen ill. At the time, in Sweden, general tests weren't available to see if they were infected with the COVID-19 virus, but Greta was pretty sure they'd had it, and she warned people to follow government guidelines.

A vaccine was going to take a long time to produce, so to make sure the disease didn't spread too quickly, governments across the world began taking steps to try to prevent people from getting sick. Schools and businesses were closed, and many people worked and studied from home to avoid contact with others.

Greta cancelled the Fridays For Future strikes, but campaigning continued online. Supporters posted photos of themselves with their climate change poster wherever they were, and numbers continued to build. By April 2020, Fridays For Future had nearly **fourteen million followers**.

The pandemic was terrible, but there were a few positive outcomes for the environment. For example:

In northern India, air pollution disappeared, and for the first time in nearly thirty years, residents in the city of Jalandhar were able to see the Dhauladhar mountain range 120 miles away!

Who put that mountain there?

🌳 Without constant boat traffic, the water in the canals of Venice, Italy, cleared. Its fish populations started to flourish and could be seen in the water for the first time in decades.

🌳 In Milan, Italy, traffic congestion dropped by up to 75% and air pollution fell too. After the outbreak the city announced plans to reduce motorized transport, widen pavements, and install bike lanes.

When governments understood there was a crisis, **they were able to act**. Now they needed to understand that another crisis was happening at the very same time as the virus. In fact, it's still happening, and the consequences could be far worse.

No Simple Solution

Whatever happens, one thing is for certain: **Greta won't stop campaigning** until we stop burning fossil fuels. And even then, there's plenty of work to be done to stop global warming as much as possible. Politicians like to talk, and they can say a lot of good things. But it's what actually happens that's important.

At the moment, many of the world's richer countries have the ingredients to do the right thing for climate change, but they're not doing it because it's going to cost a lot of money. But the cost of not making changes will be MUCH greater. The main problem is that most countries of the world concentrate on growing their economies and getting richer all the time.

We're in a system where most people think getting richer is the goal, but that mindset needs to be changed.

There's no simple solution but if governments admit there is a climate crisis, there are many ways the world could change for the better by 2030.

There's only one Planet Earth, and the resources on it are all we have. If we all come together, we can make governments change.

There's plenty you can do to help!

Keep listening to the science about climate change and encourage other people to do the same.

Join in putting pressure on companies and governments to change their policies.

Try talking to older friends and family members about using their vote to get people who will act for the climate into power.

Get involved in local projects that will help the climate crisis. Join organizations and go on protests, such as the Fridays For Future marches.

The one thing we need more than hope is action. Once we start to act, hope is everywhere.

We don't have much time!

TIMELINE

2011
Greta learns about climate change at school.

2011–2018
Greta starts finding out about the climate crisis. She becomes increasingly concerned about it and follows international climate-related events, such as the COP21 UN Conference in 2015.

| 2003

| May 2018

| July 2018

January 3, 2003
Greta is born in Stockholm, Sweden.

May 2018
Greta writes an essay about climate change that wins a competition in a Swedish newspaper.

Extinction Rebellion (XR) climate crisis organization is founded.

July 2018
Greta visits the Swedish Polar Research Secretariat, to learn about climate change in the Arctic.

August 20, 2018
Greta's School Strike for the Climate begins, as Greta strikes alone.

September 14, 2018
Greta begins the weekly #FridaysForFuture strikes, which soon spread around the world.

October 31, 2018
Greta speaks at an XR Declaration of Rebellion event in London.

| September 2018

| November 2018

September 7, 2018
The last day of the strike. By this point, more than 1,000 people have joined Greta.

November 2018
Greta gives a TED talk on the climate crisis (and becomes one of the youngest TED speakers ever).

September 8, 2018
Greta joins the People's Climate March in Stockholm and addresses the strikers in a televised speech, urging people around the world to protest.

February 21, 2019
Greta addresses politicians at the European Economic and Social Committee in Brussels.

January 25, 2019
Greta gives a speech at the World Economic Forum in Davos, Switzerland, where she meets her hero, Jane Goodall.

| December 2018 | February 2019 | April 2019 |

April 2019
Greta meets the Pope and speaks to him about climate change.

April 23, 2019
Greta addresses the UK parliament, criticizing its plans to expand airports and its use of fossil fuels.

December 2018
Greta makes a speech about the climate crisis in Poland at the United Nations Climate Change Conference (COP24) in Katowice.

May 30, 2019

Some of Greta's speeches are published in the book *No One Is Too Small to Make a Difference*.

June 2019

Greta leaves school.

July 2019

The 1975 release a song featuring Greta speaking about the climate crisis.

| June 2019

| August 2019

August 14, 2019

Greta and her dad begin their journey from Plymouth, England, to New York, via solar-powered yacht.

August 28, 2019

The yacht sails into New York harbour escorted by seventeen UN sailing boats.

Aboard La Vagabonde

September 2019

Greta meets President Barack Obama.

Greta gives a speech at the United States Congress.

Jellyfish, yum!

November 2019
Greta becomes Waterstones' Author of the Year.

September 20, 2019
The biggest climate protest to date: four million children and workers take action in 150 countries. Greta strikes in New York, with around 250,000 others.

November 13, 2019
After the Climate Change Conference (COP25) suddenly relocates from Chile to Spain, Greta and her dad set off to sail from America to Portugal, with an Australian couple and their baby.

| October 2019 | December 2019 | February 2020

October 2019
The *Nelloptodes gretae* beetle is named after Greta by London's Natural History Museum.

December 2019
Greta is named *Time* Person of the Year (and is the youngest person ever to win this honor).

February 2020
Greta meets Malala Yousafzai who is also an activist.

March 2020

Over thirteen million people in 7,500 cities strike as part of Fridays For Future.

Greta and her dad become ill with what Greta believes is COVID-19.

In-person Fridays For Future strikes are canceled due to the coronavirus pandemic, but campaigning continues online.

November 2020

Joe Biden is elected 46th president of the United States, defeating climate-change denier, Donald Trump.

| October 2020 | January 2021 | April 2021

October 2020

I Am Greta, a documentary film about Greta's life and her activism is launched.

January 2021

Greta turns eighteen.

April 2021

The BBC launches a TV series called *Greta Thunberg: A Year to Change the World*.

We need to act. NOW!

GLOSSARY

activist: Someone who campaigns to bring about social or political change.

advocate: Someone who supports a cause or a plan of action and recommends it to others.

atmosphere: The mass of gases that surround Earth.

carbon/carbon dioxide (CO_2): Carbon is an important chemical element that is found in all plants, animals and humans. When fossil fuels, such as coal, oil and gas, are burned, they release the carbon they contain back into the atmosphere as CO_2 which is a greenhouse gas.

carbon footprint:  The amount of CO_2 released into the atmosphere as a result of one person or group's activity.

chemical weapon: A chemical that can be used to inflict harm on humans.

civil war: A war between people who live in the same country.

climate change: Long-term changes to global or regional climate or weather patterns, caused by increased levels of CO_2 in the atmosphere.

conservationist: Someone who supports or acts for the protection and preservation of wildlife and the natural environment.

delegate: Someone who attends a conference on behalf of the organization they work for.

drought: A long period of unusually low rainfall, which leads to a shortage of water.

ecological: To do with the relationships between living organisms (animals/plants) and the area they live in.

environment: The natural world.

emission: When a gas is released into the atmosphere.

Eurovision: An annual international singing competition that mainly involves European countries.

extinct: When no members of a species are left alive.

flotilla: A small fleet of boats.

fossil fuel: Fuel made by burning the remains of animals and plants that died millions of years ago. Burning fossil fuels, such as gas and oil, provides much of the world's energy.

freight train: A train that transports goods (for example, food or vehicles) rather than people.

glacier: A huge mass of ice that covers a large area of land.

greenhouse gases: Gases in Earth's atmosphere that trap heat and make the planet hotter. They include CO_2 and methane.

habitat: The area where an animal or plant lives or grows.

hydroelectricity:
Electricity produced by
generators that
are pushed by
the movement
of water.

Industrial Revolution: The period
in history when there was a major and
rapid change in how things were made;
instead of goods and clothes being made
by hand in small workshops, they were
produced faster and more cheaply by
machines in factories.

IPCC: Intergovernmental Panel on
Climate Change: an organization that
assesses the science related to climate
change.

landslide: A collapse of a mass of rock
or earth from a cliff or mountain.

leach: To wash away.

LGBTQ+: Lesbian, gay, bisexual,
transgender, queer, and more: the
words different people use to describe
themselves in terms of their romantic/
sexual attraction and gender.

microbead: A tiny plastic particle.

mineral: A solid substance formed
naturally in the earth, such as copper,
iron or calcium.

narwhal: A small Arctic whale
with a large spiralling
tusk —it's
sometimes
known
as the
unicorn of
the sea.

Nobel Peace Prize: An incredibly
prestigious international award, given
to people thought to have significantly
encouraged international peace and
cooperation.

permafrost soil: A layer of sand,
gravel and soil that is permanently
frozen under the earth.

policy: A set of plans or ideas
that influence decisions,
particularly in
business, politics or
economics.

pollution: The introduction of harmful
materials into the environment; for
example, smoke and dust can create air
pollution.

refugee: Someone forced to leave their
country to escape natural disaster, war,
or unfair treatment.

renewable energy: Energy from a
source that will never be used up, such
as wind.

sediment: Small particles that gather
together, usually at the bottom of a
liquid.

solar power: Power produced by using
the energy of the sun's rays.

summit: A meeting between different
governments.

turbine: A machine that has a rotary
(spinning) engine and produces power.

United Nations: An international
organization that aims to maintain peace
and security around the world.

Notes

19   "All we have . . . and change." Greta Thunberg, "The disarming case to act right now on climate change," *TED* video, 11:03, November 2018. See ted.com/talks/greta_thunberg_the_disarming_case_to_act_right_now_on_climate_change.

23   "Warmer Climate . . . in the Air." Waldemar Kaempffert, "SCIENCE IN REVIEW: Warmer Climate on the Earth May Be Due to More Carbon Dioxide in the Air," *New York Times*, October 28, 1956. See nytimes.com/1956/10/28/archives/science-in-review-warmer-climate-on-the-earth-may-be-due-to-more.html.

25   "All this . . . the solutions." We Canada, "Severn Cullis-Suzuki at Rio Summit 1992," YouTube video, 8:31, August 16, 2012. See youtube.com/watch?v=oJJGuIZVfLM&t=115s.

45   "You just . . . people in Senegal!" Malena Ernman, "Malena Ernman on daughter Greta Thunberg: 'She was slowly disappearing into some kind of darkness.'" *Guardian*, February 23, 2020. See theguardian.com/environment/2020/feb/23/great-thunberg-malena-ernman-our-house-is-on-fire-memoir-extract.

49   "Act . . . and depression." Emma Brockes, "When Alexandria Ocasio-Cortez met Greta Thunbger: 'Hope is contagious,'" *Guardian*, June 29, 2019. See theguardian.com/environment/2019/jun/29/alexandria-ocasio-cortez-met-greta-thunberg-hope-contagious-climate.

51   "I have Asperger's . . . #aspiepower." Greta Thuberg, Twitter post, August 31, 2019, 5:44 pm. See twitter.com/gretathunberg/status/1167916177927991296?lang=en.

53   "If I would . . . a different perspective." Leslie Hook, "Greta Thunberg: 'All my life I've been the invisible girl,'" *Financial Times*, February 22, 2019. See ft.com/content/4df1b9e6-34fb-11e9-bd3a-8b2a211d90d5.

61   "It's freezing . . . 'global warming.'" Brandon Miller and Judson Jones, "Climate is not weather: Trump continues to get the two conflated," CNN, September 16, 2020. See edition.cnn.com/2020/09/15/weather/global-warming-vs-weather-trump/index.html.

62   "a hoax . . . moneymaking industry." Tim Marcin, "What Has Trump Said About Global Warming? Eight Quotes on Climate Change as He Announces

Paris Agreement Decision," *Newsweek*, June 1, 2017. See newsweek.com/
what-has-trump-said-about-global-warming-quotes-climate-change-paris-
agreement-618898.

74 "I want to . . . human history." Amelia Tait, "Greta Thunberg: How one
teenager became the voice of the planet," *WIRED*, June 6, 2019. See wired.
co.uk/article/greta-thunberg-climate-crisis.

77 "That was . . . to two." Charlotte Alter, Suyin Haynes, and Justin Worland,
"Time 2019 Person of the Year: Greta Thunberg," *Time*. See time.com/
person-of-the-year-2019-greta-thunberg.

82 "The grown-ups . . . join in." Jan Viklund, "Greta Thunberg at People's
Climate March Sweden 2018," YouTube video, 1:59, September 13, 2018.
See youtube.com/watch?v=lgt_D-6sGHU.

83 "just so endlessly . . . feeling good." Greta Thunberg, Svante Thunberg,
Malena Ernman, and Beat Ernman, *Our House Is on Fire: Scenes of a Family
and a Planet in Crisis*. New York: Penguin, 2020 (268).

94 "We need . . . the people." Connect4Climate, "Greta Thunberg full
speech at UN Climate Change COP24 Conference," YouTube video, 3:29,
December 15, 2018. See youtube.com/watch?v=VFkQSGyeCWg.

100 "I don't want . . . Because it is." World Economic Forum, "Greta
Thunberg—Our house is on fire," YouTube video, 0:57, January 25, 2019.
See youtube.com/watch?v=4toDBD_7DWY.

101 "Some people . . . group of people." Greta Thunberg, *No One Is Too Small to
Make a Difference*. New York: Penguin, 2019 (15).

102 "You're acting . . . children." European Economic and Social Committee,
"'You're acting like spoiled, irresponsible children—Speech by Greta
Thunberg, climate activist," YouTube video, 10:03, February 21, 2019. See
youtube.com/watch?v=sVeYOPJZ8oc.

104 "What's the . . . a future." Stuart McGurk, "Greta Thunberg: 'To do your
best is no longer good enough,'" *GQ*, August 12, 2019. See gq-magazine.
co.uk/men-of-the-year/article/greta-thunberg-interview.

113 "One of . . . advocates." Barack Obama, Twitter post,
September 17, 2019, 4:24 pm. See twitter.com/barackobama/
status/1174056583610949632?lang=en.

118 "How dare . . . never forgive you." United Nations, "Climate Action Summit 2019—Morning Session," YouTube video, 4:17:44, September 23, 2019. See youtube.com/watch?v=haewHZ8ubKA.

120 "I just think . . . really." Aylin Woodward, "Greta Thunberg told Ellen DeGeneres that meeting President Trump would be 'a waste of time, really,'" *Business Insider India*, November 2019. See businessinsider.in/greta-thunberg-told-ellen-degeneres-that-meeting-with-president-trump-would-be-a-waste-of-time-really/articleshow/71860262.cms.

124 "The people who . . . for change." Sebastian Kettley, "Greta Thunberg UN speech in FULL: Read climate activist's condemnation of world leaders," *Express*, December 13, 2019. See express.co.uk/news/science/1216452/Greta-Thunberg-UN-speech-full-COP25-Greta-Thunberg-speech-transcript-climate-change.

129 "So ridiculous . . . Chill!" Chris Cillizza, "We should all be appalled by Donald Trump's tweet about Greta Thunberg," CNN, December 13, 2019. See edition.cnn.com/2019/12/12/politics/greta-thunberg-donald-trump/index.html.

129 "A teenager . . . a friend." Cillizza, "We should all be appalled."

129 "He seems . . . to see." Greta Thunberg, Twitter post, January 20, 2021, 8:54 pm. See twitter.com/GretaThunberg/status/1351890941087522820.

130 "You have . . . We all are." "When Greta Thunberg met David Attenborough," BBC video, 11:37, December 30, 2019. See bbc.co.uk/programmes/p07ysljz.

131 "I truly believe . . . our souls." Yousafzai, Malala, "Library of Birmingham inauguration speech," Birmingham City Council, September 3, 2013. See birmingham.gov.uk/info/50132/visiting_the_library_of_birmingham/1600/library_of_birmingham_inauguration_speech.

132 "She's the . . . school for." "Greta Thunberg and Malala Yousafzai meet at Oxford University," *Guardian*, February 25, 2020. theguardian.com/uk-news/2020/feb/25/greta-thunberg-and-malala-yousafzai-meet-at-oxford-university.

139 "The one . . . is everywhere." Thunberg, "The disarming case."

BIBLIOGRAPHY

Alter, Charlotte, Suyin Haynes, and Justin Worland. *"Time* 2019 Person of the Year: Greta Thunberg." *Time.* See time.com/person-of-the-year-2019-greta-thunberg.

Brockes, Emma. "When Alexandria Ocasio-Cortez met Greta Thunberg: 'Hope is contagious.'" *Guardian,* June 29, 2019. See theguardian.com/environment/2019/jun/29/alexandria-ocasio-cortez-met-greta-thunberg-hope-contagious-climate.

Ernman, Malena. "Malena Ernman on daughter Greta Thunberg: 'She was slowly disappearing into some kind of darkness.'" *Guardian,* February 23, 2020. See theguardian.com/environment/2020/feb/23/great-thunberg-malena-ernman-our-house-is-on-fire-memoir-extract.

Hook, Leslie. "Greta Thunberg: 'All my life I've been the invisible girl.'" *Financial Times,* February 22, 2019. See ft.com/content/4df1b9e6-34fb-11e9-bd3a-8b2a211d90d5.

Marcin, Tim. "What Has Trump Said About Global Warming? Eight Quotes on Climate Change as He Announces Paris Agreement Decision." *Newsweek,* June 1, 2017. See newsweek.com/what-has-trump-said-about-global-warming-quotes-climate-change-paris-agreement-618898.

McGurk, Stuart. "Greta Thunberg: 'To do your best is no longer good enough.'" *GQ,* August 12, 2019. See gq-magazine.co.uk/men-of-the-year/article/greta-thunberg-interview.

Tait, Amelia. "Greta Thunberg: How one teenager became the voice of the planet." *WIRED,* June 6, 2019. See wired.co.uk/article/greta-thunberg-climate-crisis.

Thunberg, Greta. *No One Is Too Small to Make a Difference.* New York: Penguin, 2019.

Thunberg, Greta. "The disarming case to act right now on climate change." *TED* video, 11:03. November 2018. See ted.com/talks/greta_thunberg_the_disarming_case_to_act_right_now_on_climate_change.

Thunberg, Greta, Svante Thunberg, Malena Ernman, and Beat Ernman. *Our House Is on Fire: Scenes of a Family and a Planet in Crisis.* New York: Penguin, 2020.

INDEX

Use these pages for a quick reference!

Greta, you're an inspiration.

About the Author

Tracey Turner is an author and editor who has written more than seventy books that cover a wide range of topics, including famous writers, breakthrough inventions, and deadly perils. She lives in Bath, England, with her partner and son.

About the Illustrator

Tom Knight is an illustrator and writer. When not drawing, he can be found trying to play various musical instruments or staring out at a boat in his front garden that he wishes he knew how to fix. He lives in England with his wife, Tabby, and his two sons, Archie and Seth.

GET ON A FIRST-NAME BASIS
★ WITH ALL THESE ★
FAMOUS FIGURES!